NOT OF THIS WORLD
DEVOTIONS FOR YOUTH MINISTRY

Group®
Loveland, Colorado
www.group.com

Not of This World Devotions for Youth Ministry

Visit our Web site: **www.group.com**

Credits

Contributing Authors: Rick Beno, Tammy L. Bicket, Dawn M. Brandon, Heather A. Eades, Kate S. Holburn, Scott M. Kinner, Joy-Elizabeth F. Lawrence, Michael McConnell, James W. Miller, Christina Schofield, Alison Simpson, and Roxanne Wieman
Editor: Kate S. Holburn
Copy Editor: Jessica Broderick
Acquisitions Editor: Kelli B. Trujillo
Creative Development Editor: Mikal Keefer
Chief Creative Officer: Joani Schultz
Senior Art Director: Jeff A. Storm
Cover Art Director/Designer: Jeff A. Storm
Cover Illustrator: Mike Kasun
Interior Design: Liz Malwitz Design
Illustrations: Liz Malwitz, Havanna Street, and RetroAdArt.com
Production Manager: Dodie Tipton
Photography: Photodisc and Retro Americana

Library of Congress Cataloging-in-Publication Data

Not of this world devotions for youth ministry.-- 1st American pbk. ed.
p. cm.
ISBN 0-7644-2751-2 (pbk. : alk. paper)
1. Youth--Prayer-books and devotions--English. I. Group Publishing.
BV4531.3.N68 2004
268'.433--dc22
2004020848

10 9 8 7 6 5 4 3 2 1 14 13 12 11 10 09 08 07 06 05

Printed in the United States of America.

Introduction 4
Not of This World Devotions
Devotion 1: ***You-ness*** *(identity)* 5
Devotion 2: ***What's the Big Deal With Baal?*** *(God's power)* 6
Devotion 3: ***How's My Faith-Sharing? Call...*** *(sharing faith)* 7
Devotion 4: ***The High Cost of Living*** *(sin)* 8
Devotion 5: ***Friendly News*** *(friendship)*....9
Devotion 6: ***Is That a Face or a Mask?*** *(faith)* 10
Devotion 7: ***That's Incredible!*** *(Stephen/living for God)*....11
Devotion 8: ***A Vast Expanse*** *(God's sovereignty)* 12
Devotion 9: ***E-mail to an Enemy*** *(loving others)*....13
Devotion 10: ***Clean Your Room!*** *(Christian living)* 14
Devotion 11: ***From Scandal to Faith*** *(redemption)*....15
Devotion 12: ***No Gift Receipt Required*** *(spiritual gifts)* 16
Devotion 13: ***The Real Thing?*** *(sex)* 17
Devotion 14: ***The Problem of Pain*** *(suffering)*.... 18
Devotion 15: ***Father and Child*** *(God the Father)*.... 19
Devotion 16: ***The Fast Lane*** *(fasting)* 20
Devotion 17: ***Thank God!*** *(service)* 21
Devotion 18: ***Scenes From a Mall*** *(parents)*....22
Devotion 19: ***Unexpected Friendship*** *(friendship)* 23
Devotion 20: ***So How Human Was Jesus?*** *(Jesus)* 24
Devotion 21: ***Surprise Birthday Party*** *(Joseph/trusting God)*....25
Devotion 22: ***Stay Close*** *(friendship with Jesus)* 26
Devotion 23: ***Odd Couples*** *(faith and science)*.... 27
Devotion 24: ***Two Kings*** *(injustice/living for God)* 28
Devotion 25: ***It's the Little Things That Count*** *(God's omniscience)* 29
Devotion 26: ***Following the Leader*** *(sharing faith)* 30
Devotion 27: ***Messages From God*** *(Ezekiel/trusting God)*....31
Devotion 28: ***Dating the Best Way*** *(dating)* 32
Devotion 29: ***God's GPS*** *(accountability)* 33
Devotion 30: ***Can You Hear Me Now?*** *(prayer)*....34
Devotion 31: ***How to Know More Than You Thought You Did*** *(the Holy Spirit)*..35
Devotion 32: ***Multiple-Choice Service*** *(service)* 36
Devotion 33: ***Career Detour*** *(following God)*....38
Devotion 34: ***Rebellious Images*** *(self-image)*....39
Devotion 35: ***Why It's Good to Be a Clown*** *(glorifying God)*....40
Devotion 36: ***Three Days, Two Voices*** *(the Gospel)*....41
Devotion 37: ***The Loners*** *(Christian fellowship)* 42
Devotion 38: ***True Enough*** *(truth about Jesus)*....43
Devotion 39: ***Extra! Extra! Read All About It!*** *(Rahab/serving God)* 44
Devotion 40: ***Out of Love and Obedience*** *(drugs and alcohol)*....45
Devotion 41: ***Bible Camp S.O.S.*** *(sharing faith)*....46
Devotion 42: ***Biker Followers*** *(God's love)* 48
Devotion 43: ***Retired Man Saves Raspberries*** *(helping others)* 49
Devotion 44: ***Tell the Truth*** *(honesty)*....50
Devotion 45: ***(Interesting) Ways to Use Your Old Stuff*** *(God's creation)*....51
Devotion 46: ***What's Up With Hell?*** *(hell)* 52
Devotion 47: ***The Unknown God*** *(sharing faith)* 53
Devotion 48: ***Lost Opportunity*** *(loving others)* 54
Devotion 49: ***Is That You?*** *(Elijah/hearing God)*....56
Devotion 50: ***Prejudice Is a Drag*** *(prejudice)* 57
Devotion 51: ***The Price of Freedom*** *(St. Francis/living for God)* 58
Devotion 52: ***Can't Wait!*** *(Jesus' return)*....59

Introduction

The night before he died on the cross, Jesus prayed, "I have given them your word and the world has hated them, for they are not of the world any more than I am of the world. My prayer is not that you take them out of the world but that you protect them from the evil one. They are not of the world, even as I am not of it. Sanctify them by the truth; your word is truth. As you sent me into the world, I have sent them into the world" (John 17:14-18).

It's sometimes challenging for Christian teenagers to understand what it means to "not be of the world," especially when they're living in it! *Not of This World Devotions for Youth Ministry* offers fifty-two devotions that will help your students both understand *and* live this out in their everyday lives. They'll take a fresh look at God's amazing love for them, explore what it means to be a Christian, dig into the wonderful truths of the Bible, and grow deeper in their relationships with Jesus. Check out what each **photocopiable devotion flier** has that will help your students be "not of this world"!

- **A devotion** that focuses on a topic relevant to students. There are devotions about relationships with friends, family, and the opposite sex; devotions about Jesus and God's Word; devotions about people who were committed to living for God no matter what; devotions about what it means to grow as a Christian in today's world; devotions about tough spiritual questions; and on and on!
- **A key Scripture** that reveals what God's Word says about the topic.
- **A Daily Challenge™** that gives teenagers a specific opportunity to practice their faith.
- **A cool quote** that connects to the devotion theme.
- **"My Thoughts" and "My Prayers"** sections where students can journal about what God is teaching them and how they would like to grow closer to Jesus.

Read on for some ways you can use *Not of This World Devotions* in your youth ministry.

- Photocopy and distribute the same devotion flier to all your students at one time, and go through devotion and journaling together. Encourage students to carry out the Daily Challenge during the week. Do the same with another devotion flier the following week, and so on.
- Photocopy and distribute the same devotion flier to all your students, and encourage them to go through the devotion, journaling, and Daily Challenge on their own during the week. Do the same with another devotion flier the following week, and so on.
- Photocopy and distribute a different devotion flier to each student at one time, and encourage everyone to go through the devotion, journaling, and Daily Challenge during the week. The next time you meet together, have everyone share his or her individual experience.

Not of This World Devotions is powerful, life-changing, and easy to use. Use your imagination and creativity to help your teenagers grow in their relationships with Jesus and understand how they can be "not of this world"!

"I should hardly admire [snowflakes] more if real stars fell and lodged on my coat."
—HENRY DAVID THOREAU

You-ness

If you were a snowflake, you would be put into a category such as "capped column," "spatial dendrite," "stellar dendrite," and "needle." But even with these classifications, no two individual snowflakes (more rightly called snow crystals) are alike. Think about it. Of the millions of snowflakes...no, billions of...no, countless snowflakes that have fallen over time, two have never been exactly the same. Snowflakes form when water vapor freezes around tiny particles of pollution, dust, or salt in the air. And as a snowflake falls, it is changed and influenced by air currents, humidity, wind speed, and much more. All these factors help create a snowflake that is unique and one of a kind.

You are one of a kind too—specially designed by God to be unique! And just like the snowflake, you are influenced and changed by things in your life, such as family, friends, school, church, and experiences. All these things contribute to your unique you—call it your "you-ness."

And since only you are you (are you following?), only you can do some of the great things that God wants. You have been uniquely made, and God wants to uniquely use you to fulfill his purposes in your life and in the lives of others. So embrace your "you-ness" and your special place in God's plan!

You have been uniquely made!

MY THOUGHTS:

"I am fearfully and wonderfully made."
—Psalm 139:14a

MY PRAYERS:

DAILY Challenge™

Using scissors and some folded white paper, create a unique snowflake for yourself. Write your name on it, and hang it where you will see it every day. Each time you do, thank God for making you uniquely you!

What's the Big Deal With Baal?

"When you realize that there is an Almighty God on whom you can rely, it provides a great comfort."
—GEORGE W. BUSH

Special effects are cool. If you use a DVD player, chances are that the action flick you rent has a bit about the movie's special effects in the "special features" option. It's always amazing to see how movies are created on a set. Then when you see the movie, everything looks so different and, well, real. The people who work in special effects must have so much fun at their jobs! They get to create explosions, car chases, people that aren't really there, and on and on.

But we need to remember that the display of power in the Bible happened way before special effects were ever dreamed of. If the Bible came out on DVD, you could see God send down a bonfire to consume Elijah's offering (1 Kings 18:16-40). It was 100 percent real, and it *meant* something. And it definitely caught people's attention.

In the story, it was Baal versus God. Elijah challenged the Baal worshippers to a fire duel of sorts. Everyone showed up at Mount Carmel for the show. But when the Baal worshippers sacrificed their bull to Baal, nothing happened. Then Elijah got his bull ready on the altar to God and even poured water over it three times. He prayed to God, and the fire fell on the altar, burned up everything, and even "licked up the water in the trench" (verse 38). Now, in our special effects world, we'd probably stare at the screen and wonder, "How'd they do that?" But when the people in the story saw it, they were astounded and fell to the ground, worshipping God.

One of the "special effects" of God's power is that as Christians, it's not scary to us. It's actually a comfort that such a powerful God loves us and can be trusted at every moment of our lives. And on the Bible DVD, every special feature we'd see would express God's love for us. It's the thread that runs through every story and a truth we should always remember.

MY THOUGHTS:

"Because of the Lord's great love we are not consumed, for his compassions never fail. They are new every morning; great is your faithfulness."
—Lamentations 3:22-23

MY PRAYERS:

Go for a walk, and look for displays of God's power and the ways his power influences life. Say a prayer of thanks and praise for the beauty and grace of God's power.

How's My Faith-Sharing? Call...

Ever seen those religious bumper stickers? They show different ways to share your faith. Here are a few.

- Friendly: "Come on over to my place! –God"
- Aggressive: "My God can beat up your God!"
- Subtle: Just a fish
- Funny: "My boss is a Jewish carpenter."
- Hard for outsiders to understand: "In the event of rapture, car will swerve out of control."
- Easy to understand: "Jesus loves you."

These show us a bunch of ways to share our faith, to do "evangelism." The word *evangelism* has Greek roots and just means sharing good (*eu*) news (*angellion*, like *angel* or *messenger*). Telling other people about Jesus is just a matter of telling them good news. Not *all* the ways listed above are good for everyone, but there is some way that's good for you to share your faith.

It could be friendly: "Wanna see how cool my youth group is?" Or it could be the right comforting words at the right time to a friend in need: "Sometimes when I feel alone, I turn to God." Maybe your sense of humor will kick in: "You sure say 'God' a lot. Would you like me to introduce you?"

Figure out what your way is...and maybe make a bumper sticker!

"Killing Jesus was like trying to destroy a dandelion seed-head by blowing on it."
–WALTER WINK

MY THOUGHTS:

"Therefore go and make disciples of all nations, baptizing them in the name of the Father and of the Son and of the Holy Spirit."
–Matthew 28:19

MY PRAYERS:

Survey your friends by asking them these questions:
(1) What do you believe about God?
(2) Why are some people religious?
(3) What are the best ways to find out more about God? If they ask *you* questions, tell them the good news!

The High Cost of Living

Aron Ralston had a passion for the outdoors. Experienced and competent, Ralston had successfully climbed forty-nine of Colorado's highest mountains.

On Saturday, April 26, 2003, the mountaineer embarked on a thirteen-mile, one-day rock climb in Utah's remote and difficult Bluejohn Canyon. But disaster struck when his right hand and forearm were pinned by an 800-pound boulder. He couldn't budge the rock, and there was little chance he would be rescued: He had broken his own first rule by not telling anyone where he was going.

Three liters of water lasted only until Tuesday. By Thursday, Ralston realized he wouldn't survive without drastic measures to free himself. He would amputate his own arm. With grim determination, he first broke the bones, then used his pocketknife to cut through skin and tendons. Then Ralston rappelled sixty-six feet down the canyon and walked three hours before rescuers found him.

Ralston loved something that, no matter how enjoyable, held potential dangers. While the boulder falling on his arm was an accident, with greater care and accountability (telling people where he was going and when he'd be back), Ralston could have increased his odds of being rescued with both hands intact.

Mountain climbing can be dangerous, but it's neither positive nor negative spiritually. However, many people subject themselves needlessly to the dangers of sin. Are you at risk of being crushed by sin? Maybe you're unwilling to give up a harmful relationship that's leading you farther from God. Maybe you're unconscious to the trap of violent music or video games. Perhaps you didn't anticipate the boulder of temptation that certain Web sites would unleash. You may think you can flirt with danger and break God's first rule—holiness.

Watch out! The time may come when a boulder of sin lands squarely on you, threatening your spiritual existence—or your life. But you can prevent sin from trapping and destroying you with Aron Ralston's kind of courage and clear thinking. Confess to Jesus and draw close to him. Recognize the danger and take drastic action, when necessary, to save yourself. Release yourself from the weight of sin. Cut it off! Let Jesus set you free.

"What you don't do can be a destructive force."
—ELEANOR ROOSEVELT

MY THOUGHTS:

"Let us throw off everything that hinders and the sin that so easily entangles, and let us run with perseverance the race marked out for us."
—Hebrews 12:1

Hike somewhere alone (as Aron did, but not somewhere dangerous!). Seriously consider which habits, loves, addictions, relationships, or thought patterns are weighing you down and damaging you. What will you do to free yourself from these destructive things?

Friendly News

"Good evening. This is the news, and I'm your newscaster, Gabby Maximus. We are bringing you a special report this evening on a book titled *Good Friends,* by renowned sociologist Barry Smart. Dr. Smart is joining us live on the program. Good evening, Dr. Smart."

"Good evening, Gabby."

"Is it fair to summarize your book by saying that it is best to pick friends who will be a benefit to you and not a burden? And, may I say, I personally live that way."

"That is a fair summary, Gabby."

"Your book gave me...I mean...someone I know the courage to dispose of some worthless friends. I...um... she knew someone who thought she should be a friend just because she was family! Can you believe it?"

"That's unfortunate, Gabby."

"You're telling me. I told my sister to take a hike."

"No! I mean, unfortunately, my research since writing the book seems to indicate that my book is wrong. It seems that basing friendship on personal benefit leads to short-lived and unfulfilling relationships. This lack of meaningful relationships has actually made people miserable."

"Are you saying, Dr. Smart, that this is a reason that I... I mean other people have no lasting friendships and become miserable?"

"Yes, Gabby."

"Well, that explains a lot. You know...about other people."

"There is good news, however, Gabby. My research did confirm the teachings on friendship found in another book. The Bible teaches that people should seek to help others. Then, from that behavior, healthy friendships will grow. The book even has an example character, Jesus, who lived that very way and developed eternal friendships."

"Wow! I want that kind of meaningful life! I mean, that concludes our special report on *Good Friends,* by Dr. B. Smart. By the way, don't buy it. You may want to check out that Bible book instead. Good evening."

Making good friends is not always easy. But perhaps we need to have the right motivation. Should making friends be the result of seeking benefit for ourselves? Or should making friends be the result of bestowing benefit on others? Check out what that Bible book says!

"Let us develop a kind of dangerous unselfishness."
—MARTIN LUTHER KING JR.

MY THOUGHTS:

Think of one friend. Make a list of the good things going on in your friend's life. Make another list of the bad things. Do something for him or her that will either add to the good or take away from the bad.

"My command is this: Love each other as I have loved you. Greater love has no one than this, that he lay down his life for his friends."
—John 15:12-13

Is That a Face or a Mask?

In pottery class at school, Melinda had made and decorated a beautiful, intricate teapot for her mother's birthday. The night before the celebration, Melinda dreamed that she presented the teapot—beautifully wrapped—to her mother. After opening the gift, her mother said, "Melinda, you make the ugliest things. You know I don't even drink tea!" Then she stood up, pitched the teapot at the wall, and ripped off a rubber mask. The woman Melinda had known as "Mom" her entire life wasn't who she thought she was! She was a mean, cruel person, giving fake affection and love for years in order to win Melinda's trust so that she could one day reveal her true identity. Melinda awoke, breathless, and ran into her mother's room. "Mom, I dreamed you weren't you—you were just faking that you loved me, and you really wanted to hurt me!"

A lot of times, it's easy to wonder if the people who say and act like they love us really do. Even if the love looks real, what if it's a lie, just like Melinda's mom in her dream? There are signs that seem to point to the existence of love, but we can't really prove it. We have to trust that it's real. After her dream, Melinda had to continue to trust her mom—and that there wasn't some scary non-mom hiding under a mask.

Believing in the love of other people is, in some ways, like belief in God. We can't prove either one. We can point to indicators, but we can't prove without a shadow of a doubt. In Scripture, though, there is little talk of proof in relation to faith. Though Christian apologists may give twenty reasons to believe in the existence of God, no one can pull God out of a backpack to pass around at school. That would be proof (and a little weird!), but that's not what faith is about. It's about what we don't see and, sometimes, what we don't understand.

"If there is a God of infinite goodness, and he justly deserves my allegiance and faith, I risk doing the greatest injustice by not acknowledging him."
—PETER KREEFT and RONALD K. TACELLI

MY THOUGHTS:

"Now faith is being sure of what we hope for and certain of what we do not see." —Hebrews 11:1

MY PRAYERS:

We have faith in many things we don't understand, such as traffic lights, running water, and love from friends and family. Make a list of people or things you interact with every day that require you to have faith. Consider what would happen if you suddenly started to question these things.

"I don't think I'm going to be recognized as I go down the street."
—MICHAEL SHAFER (MICHIGAN STATE UNIVERSITY GRAD STUDENT WHO DISCOVERED THE LARGEST-KNOWN PRIME NUMBER)

That's Incredible!

Check out these amazing facts and feats.

• The longest-reigning monarch was King Louis XIV of France, who was *five years old* when he ascended the throne. He reigned as king for seventy-two years, from 1643-1715.

• The youngest Oscar award winner ever was Shirley Temple, who won a special award for "outstanding contribution during 1934" in the 1934 Academy Awards. She was six years old.

• Want to make some money? Brush up on your golf swing. The PGA golfer with the highest winning earnings in 2002 was Tiger Woods, who earned $7,392,188 from PGA Tour wins.

It's funny how some people are remembered in life. Have you ever thought about how you might be remembered? It's not the happiest thought, but give it a try. How do you want to be remembered?

The end of a guy named Stephen's life is told in Acts 6:8-8:1a. He's remembered as a martyr, a word that can sometimes have a negative meaning. People talk about martyrs being crazy, or victims, or attention-seekers. But Stephen was the real deal. He lived his life for Christ, and he died preaching the message of hope and grace. In fact, he died because of his loyalty to Jesus. Stephen is an incredible example of strength and commitment.

You can make the same kind of statement with the way you live your life. Don't miss the beautiful opportunity to show God's love in the way you live! Remember to live your life so that those who see you are seeing God's love.

MY THOUGHTS:

"How great is the love the Father has lavished on us, that we should be called children of God!"
—1 John 3:1a

MY PRAYERS:

DAILY Challenge™

As you go through your day, take some moments to just sit and people-watch. Look for examples of God's love in the things people are doing. Say a prayer for those people, and for yourself as well, to always show God's love in everything.

A Vast Expanse

"God is not only within sight, he is within reach."
—MAX LUCADO

• There are more than 6 billion people on Earth today.

• Each person has about 100 trillion cells, and the heart beats about 3 billion times during the average person's lifetime.

• About 90 million miles separate Earth from the sun.

• Every year we travel 584,018,332 miles around the sun.

• Earth is the third planet from the sun—a perfect distance so we don't freeze or melt.

• The size and rotation of Earth are perfectly set so we don't collapse or fly off the planet.

• The sun has a diameter of 864,948 miles. It weighs 2,000 trillion trillion tons, according to Earth's standards. The temperature is 27 million degrees Fahrenheit at the core and 10,832 degrees at the surface. One inch of the sun's surface gives off the same amount of light as 650,000 candles.

• You can see about two thousand stars with only your eyes.

• If a grain of sand was the temperature of a star's nucleus—more than 60 million degrees—it would incinerate someone up to one hundred miles away.

• The Milky Way galaxy, the one we're in, contains around 100 billion stars. It is 100,000 light-years wide (it would take 100,000 years to cross the galaxy if traveling at the speed of light), and it is spinning at about 62 million mph.

• There could be 20 trillion other galaxies in the universe, each containing billions of stars, numerous solar systems, and other planets.

God created all of this, from the stars in the farthest galaxies to each individual cell in your body. They were all masterfully designed to fit into God's perfect plan. God knows everything about his universe. In fact, God intimately knows everything about you, even things you don't know about yourself!

Humans are the only beings created in God's likeness—the very image of God. He knows and loves each person. Think about how amazing that is for you: More than anything, God loves you as an individual, so much that he would lay down his life just to be with you.

MY THOUGHTS:

"O Lord, you have searched me and you know me. You know when I sit and when I rise; you perceive my thoughts from afar."
—Psalm 139:1-2

Check out God's creation—look at the stars or watch nature. While you do that, write down what God might say to you in a love letter or what you actually sense God saying to you at that moment.

MY PRAYERS:

E-mail to an Enemy

"Love conquers all."
–VIRGIL

hey! so, yeah, it is kind of weird for me to be sending you an e-mail, but i wanted to let you know a few things that i've been thinking about. i know that we haven't necessarily been getting along very well lately, and i can't say that i really know why. but i have some guesses—some of it has to do with me. i try my best to be nice to everyone, but sometimes when we get to talking, my head gets all stupid, and i start to say things I don't really mean and never wanted to say. i am not sure if i am just proud or insecure or insane or what, but i definitely find myself doing and saying things i later regret. anyway, what i am trying to say is that even though we are not really friends right now, i also don't want us to be enemies.

do you read the bible much? i have been reading it more and just finished reading a part where jesus says that we ought to love our enemies. as i said, i don't want us to be enemies, but i also know that i need to do a better job of not being such a jerk to you. i don't know how you feel about all of this, but i am going to work on treating you better, so that maybe i won't think of us as enemies anymore. maybe we can talk about it sometime? let me know. thanks. see you later.

MY THOUGHTS:

"Love your enemies."
–Matthew 5:44

MY PRAYERS:

Think of someone in your life whom you might call an "enemy." Get out a piece of paper, and brainstorm a list of kind things you could do for that person. Pick something from your list, and do it!

Clean Your Room!

"We should live our lives as though Christ were coming this afternoon."
—JIMMY CARTER

Host: Welcome to Trading Places, the room makeover show where two people switch bedrooms to completely redecorate them. Today Bob from Wisconsin and Jesus of Nazareth will be switching rooms. We've sent our crews ahead to look at each room. Let's go see what Bob and our designers found when they showed up at Jesus' room. Bob, are you there?

Bob: We're here, and apparently we just missed Jesus—his mom says he's at the temple again. She's letting us into his room to see what we have to work with.

Host: Great! Tell us what you see.

Bob: Well, we're opening the door...

Host: And taking a look around. What does it look like?

Bob: It's totally clean, that's for sure! It's very bright in here, lots of great lighting. Um, there's a Bible, a funky-looking beanbag in the corner labeled "Prayer Chair," and lots of cool posters all over the place with pictures of lovely, pure...I don't know...I guess, "excellent" things. And man! He's got a killer stereo system in here and a ton of CDs, all labeled "Dad."

Host: So, Bob. What's your prognosis? What will you and our team of experts do to revamp Jesus' room?

Bob: Well...nothing. I mean, it's perfect. After all, he is God, you know.

Host: Nothing?! Well, I must say, we've never had this happen on our show before. A perfect room! Well, let's just go see what our other crew is discovering over at Bob's house. We've tracked Jesus down, and he is with our team of experts, getting ready to open the door to Bob's bedroom.

Bob: What's that? Jesus—checking out my room?! NOOOOOOOO!!!!!!

Jesus wants to completely redecorate your "room," making a special place for his Father right there in your heart. What would he find in there right now? We are all called to keep our "rooms" clean by making them more like Jesus'. Spend some time with God in a quiet place this week. Study his Word to learn more about what Jesus' life looked like. Spend time in prayer, and ask God to reveal the areas in your life that need work. What things need to go? What things need to happen so you can draw closer to him? And then, be sure to simply be still...and listen.

MY THOUGHTS:

"I want to know Christ and the power of his resurrection and the fellowship of sharing in his sufferings, becoming like him in his death, and so, somehow, to attain to the resurrection from the dead."
—Philippians 3:10-11

MY PRAYERS:

Draw a picture of what you think God's room would look like. Post it where you can continually add things you discover about his character while studying his Word.

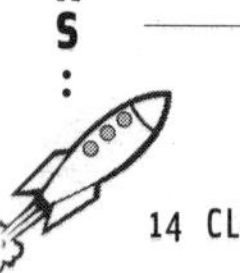

From Scandal to Faith

During the 1972 presidential campaign, police arrested five men who were bugging the Democratic Party headquarters in the Watergate office complex in Washington. Three of these five men were on the payroll of the Republican "Committee to Re-elect the President." When President Nixon denied knowledge of the break-in, the incident was *almost* swept under the carpet.

But Nixon found out shortly after that the burglars had taken orders from his own aides, and he bribed them to keep quiet while they were in jail. Two of them didn't, and the infamous Watergate scandal began. Ultimately, about forty people were charged with crimes including conspiracy, obstruction of justice, and perjury. One of these criminals was Charles Colson, special assistant to the president.

In the midst of his disappointment and deep conviction over his involvement in the Watergate scandal, Colson began a relationship with Jesus. After serving a seven-month prison sentence, he established Prison Fellowship, a ministry which focuses on sharing the love of Jesus with people in prison. He is the author of numerous books, including *Born Again,* which is the story of his conversion. Colson's life serves to remind us of the good things God can do, even when humans make mistakes.

"For Pride is spiritual cancer: it eats up the very possibility of love, or contentment, or even common sense."
—C.S. LEWIS

MY THOUGHTS:

DAILY Challenge™

Sometimes you have to leave things behind in order to follow God. What do you need to leave behind? Write some things on small pieces of paper, rip them up, and flush them down the toilet or throw them in the garbage.

" 'Come, follow me,' Jesus said, 'and I will make you fishers of men.' At once they left their nets and followed him."
—Matthew 4:19-20

MY PRAYERS:

No Gift Receipt Required

> "God's gifts put man's best dreams to shame."
> —ELIZABETH BARRETT BROWNING

When it comes to receiving gifts, we all know that it's the thought that counts. But have you ever received a gift that made you wonder what, exactly, the giver was thinking? Let's take a look at some of those infamous bad gifts.

• The Grandma Gift: We all love our grandmas. And the best gifts they can give are the times they spend sharing their "way it was" stories with us. Unfortunately, grandmas sometimes keep us in the past in other ways, such as when they get us the Noah's ark sweater vest we would've looked sooo cute in...when we were six.

• The Strangely Disappearing Gift: Maybe it was a "blue-light special." Maybe the gift-giver had done forty-eight hours of shopping without sleep. Whatever the reason for the skewed judgment, these gifts strangely disappear to the back of the closet, often without being removed from the box. Can you say "rock polisher"?

• The "Oops! I Forgot" Gift: This gift is simply the unfortunate result of forgetfulness. It is the bag of cheese curls or the travel-size dental floss from the corner gas station. It is the fuzzy frog baby that still bears the scent of the fast-food meal it came from. It is the gift that inspired the phrase "It's the thought that counts."

The good news is that God loves to give gifts—and his gifts always rock! God knows us inside and out because he created us. And with such a creative God, you are bound to receive only the most creative gifts. Spiritual gifts are God's way of equipping us for the jobs he has planned for each of us. They are specific to who we are as individuals. Not one is better than another, and they never need a gift receipt. They are gifts of the Holy Spirit to be used in serving our Father in heaven. Some of these awesome gifts include wisdom, knowledge, faith, encouragement, and teaching—all to be used for good and for God. And there's an added bonus: They come with a lifetime warranty!

MY THOUGHTS:

"Which of you fathers, if your son asks for a fish, will give him a snake instead? Or if he asks for an egg, will give him a scorpion? If you then, though you are evil, know how to give good gifts to your children, how much more will your Father in heaven give the Holy Spirit to those who ask him!"
—Luke 11:11-13

MY PRAYERS:

DAILY Challenge™

Discover the spiritual gifts that God has given you! Take a spiritual gifts test (your church or local Christian organization can provide some great ones). Then take some time to pray that God will reveal ways you can use those gifts for his glory.

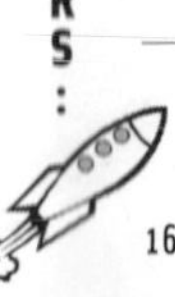

The Real Thing?

You've heard the advertising claims, and you've learned to read between the lines to figure out what advertisers are *not* telling you.

• Two out of three people prefer the taste...to motor oil.

• One-third less calories...when compared to our super-starchy jumbo version.

• Improve your complexion, and improve your life. Side effects of taking this product may include headache, nausea, muscle weakness, abnormal growth of facial hair, drooling, flatulence, or death.

Satan makes some big promises about sex outside of marriage, but he specializes in omissions, half-truths, and outright lies. The powerful images and feel-good messages about sex come from television, music, magazines, the Internet, peers, and our own hormones. Advertisers use sex to sell everything from food and clothes to deodorant.

With this bombardment, it's easy to start buying into society's attitudes toward sex. But that's dangerous. You can learn to discern Satan's lies about sex outside of marriage. Read the fine print on these claims.

• **If you have sex, you'll be popular.** You want people to love you, not what you'll do for them. People who have sex to be popular often lose their self-esteem. Hold out for true love with a spouse who wants what's best for you.

• **Everyone's doing it.** Actually, studies consistently show that the majority of teenagers are *not* having sex. And how many of those who had sex did so (or continue) because they felt pressured by the lie that everyone else was doing it?

• **If you're not having sex, something must be wrong with you.** Anyone can have sex. (Just think about all the ugly parents you've seen.) Strong, smart people—not unattractive ones—refrain from sex before marriage.

• **Having sex isn't a big deal. It doesn't hurt anyone.** Oh, really? How will your parents feel about it? How will Jesus feel? How will you feel when you and your partner break up or when the doctor gives you bad news? No matter how innocent you think sex outside of marriage is, God calls it sin. And because he loves you so much, he doesn't want sin to hurt your relationship with him or lead you to other painful consequences.

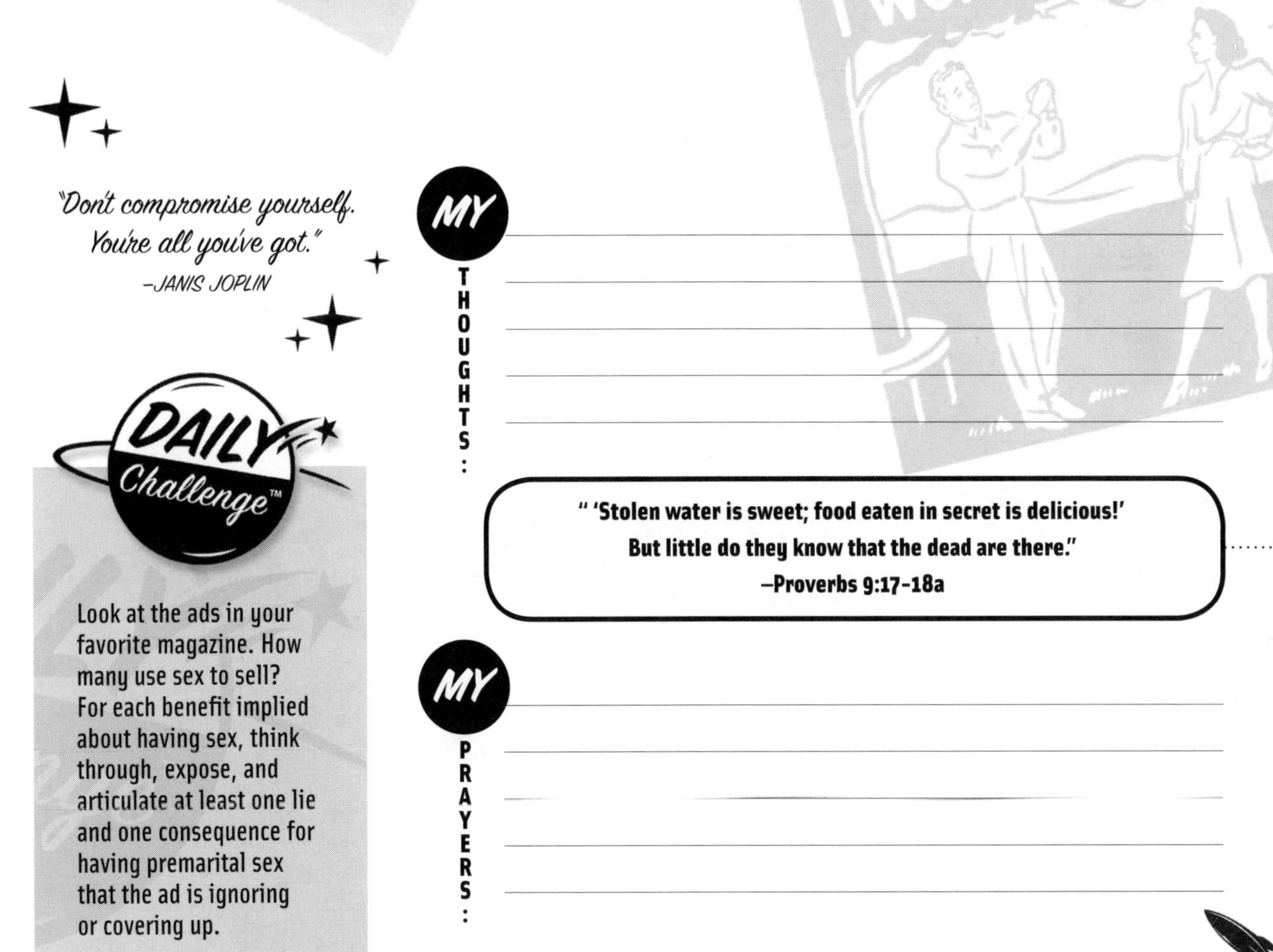

"Don't compromise yourself. You're all you've got."
—JANIS JOPLIN

MY THOUGHTS:

"'Stolen water is sweet; food eaten in secret is delicious!' But little do they know that the dead are there."
—Proverbs 9:17-18a

DAILY Challenge™

Look at the ads in your favorite magazine. How many use sex to sell? For each benefit implied about having sex, think through, expose, and articulate at least one lie and one consequence for having premarital sex that the ad is ignoring or covering up.

MY PRAYERS:

The Problem of Pain

"God...shouts in our pains: it is His megaphone to rouse a deaf world."
–C.S. LEWIS

Imagine that you have just bragged to your friends that you have been a great swimmer since before you were born...somehow. Anyway, you jump in a pool in front of them all, only to discover that you can barely stay afloat.

This is what the great Christian writer C.S. Lewis must have experienced when he went through a painful time in his life. He had written a book explaining why God let bad things happen to good people called *The Problem of Pain.* Then, late in life, he married a woman named Joy who, after only a few years of marriage, died of cancer. Lewis was terribly depressed, so much so that when a pastor told him that this was a chance to trust God, Lewis responded, "No, what we have here is a mess." His own book could not comfort him in his pain. Lewis then wrote the book *A Grief Observed,* which described his grief and struggle with God.

In the end, Lewis held onto his faith in God, and it was a much more mature faith. His second book has comforted many who have suffered through loss. (You can see his story in the movie *Shadowlands.*)

God is love and wants us to freely love him. When Adam and Eve chose to step away from him, the world became tainted with the consequences of sin. Real suffering happens. However, Jesus loves us in our suffering and wants to heal our hurts. God knows what it's like to suffer, even to the point of death.

It's OK if painful experiences confuse or depress us. But God won't leave us to our suffering. He's eager to come swimming after you when you feel as if you're in the deep end of the pool.

MY THOUGHTS:

" 'For I know the plans I have for you,' declares the Lord, 'plans to prosper you and not to harm you, plans to give you hope and a future.' "
–Jeremiah 29:11

Write a letter of encouragement to a friend who has gone through a hard time lately. Rather than trying to fix his or her problems, remember that what means the most is that you and God care for your friend.

MY PRAYERS:

Father and Child

NOVEMBER 7, 2005

What's the deal with Dad? I just don't get him, and he obviously does not get me, either. It's impossible to make him understand anything about me. He doesn't care about me, probably doesn't even love me. The way he acts, how would I ever know if he did? All that he cares about is how I messed up, what I did wrong, how I embarrassed him. Why can't he just accept me for who I am? I'm not an A student; I'm just pretty much average. But is that wrong? He's got all this pride attached to the fact that I'm his only son, and he always assumes I'm going to let him down. God, please help me. I know it's wrong to think this, but I can't wait to get out of the house so I can get away from him.

DECEMBER 25, 2013

Today might have been Dad's last Christmas with us. The news from the doctor wasn't good. The chemo didn't help, and all they can do now is make him comfortable in his remaining days. I see the emotion in his eyes, but he's so afraid to show it. Now that I'm older, I understand my dad more. He's not a bad guy. We should have talked more when I was a teenager. I think that would have helped a lot. He just wanted me to have a really good life, that's all. I can see now that he really loves me. It's funny, because in the same way that I accused him of expecting me to be perfect, I think I expected the same of him, too. No one can live up to those expectations. I expected him to be this perfect father, and that's just not possible for anyone except you, God. I thank you for being the perfect Father to both me and my dad. Thanks for helping our relationship get stronger. I just wish we had more time together now. I don't want to lose him. I love him. I want more time, God. Please, we need more time...

"The biggest thing you find out is how deep you can love. There's just an endless, bottomless well of love there."

—SINGER TIM McGRAW, ON BEING A FATHER

MY THOUGHTS:

____

____

____

____

____

____

"I will be a Father to you, and you will be my sons and daughters, says the Lord Almighty."
—2 Corinthians 6:18

Take a poll. Ask at least five people how they feel about God being our Father. Then ask yourself what it means to you to have God as your Father, and say a prayer of thanks to him for his fatherly love. Also pray for those who have difficulty seeing God as their Father.

MY PRAYERS:

____

____

____

____

____

____

The Fast Lane

RECIPE FOR FAITH

1. Find an 8x10-inch, non-greased Bible.
2. Sprinkle prayer over the pages.
3. Blend in the Holy Spirit.
4. Fast from all nonessential ingredients.
5. Surround the dish with a community of believers.
6. Garnish with good works.
7. Serve Jesus at 100 degrees Celsius.

"To be a knight of Christ one must begin with victory over one's self."
—ST. BONAVENTURE

A lot of these elements of a recipe for faith may look familiar. We know about Bible study, prayer, and service, but many people are less familiar with the spiritual discipline of fasting.

In the Bible, Jesus teaches that God rewards those who fast. Many biblical heroes would abstain from eating anything for a period of time to focus on prayer and God. Fasting is a way of taking out of our daily diets all the junk food that gets in the way of the healthy digestion of God's Word. For instance, you may ask God to give you meaning in life but then spend three hours a day watching TV—how much meaning can be found in that? Fasting is just a way of removing nonessential ingredients from your day so you can really feast on what's most important. (The word *breakfast* means you have come to the end of your fast—you "break fast" by eating again.)

When you fast, you make room for all the best things God has to give you. As Jesus says, God rewards you when you fast. Cut out the fat and grease of your life with a fast, and bake a better faith!

Holy Bible

Fresh DAILY BREAD

MY THOUGHTS:

"When you fast, put oil on your head and wash your face, so that it will not be obvious to men that you are fasting...and your Father...will reward you."
—Matthew 6:17-18

MY PRAYERS:

Starting today, choose something to fast from for the next week, such as soda, television, or something else. At the times when you'd normally concentrate on this thing, take time to pray instead.

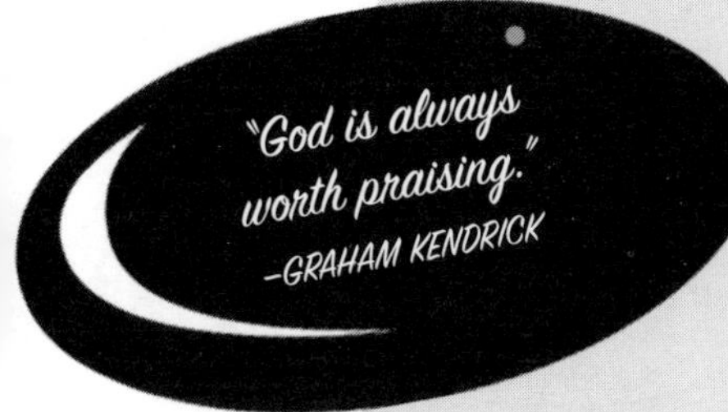

Thank God!

We often say thanks to God, at least at meal time. But there is much more we can do than just saying thanks to God. Serving others is also a great way to give a living thanks to God. Check out what these students had to say.

- **John, 18, after serving six weeks in the inner city:** "I never imagined how difficult life is for some people. Just being with them each and every day gave me a better perspective of both the great blessings God has given me but also on the responsibility I have to give to others."
- **Gretchen, 16, after serving eight weeks at a summer camp:** "God taught me so much about giving every part of myself to the campers. I always felt tired and energized at the same time. By talking to the kids and playing with them and sharing Christ with them, I knew that I was doing exactly what God wanted me to do."
- **Ally, 14, after singing in a nursing home:** "I didn't think I would like being around a lot of old people. But I learned that they have a lot to teach me. They loved us being there, and they just thanked us and thanked us. One lady thanked me and then thanked God for me. It was cool."

Want to thank God today? Find a way to serve someone else in Jesus' name.

MY THOUGHTS:

"Let us not become weary in doing good, for at the proper time we will reap a harvest if we do not give up."
–Galatians 6:9

Do a mini service project for someone this week. Here are some ideas: Shovel someone's driveway. Help someone with his or her homework. Clean your brother's room. Serve at a soup kitchen. Serve someone else as a thanksgiving to God.

MY PRAYERS:

Scenes From a Mall

OK. The second Dad stops the car at the mall, I'll bolt, lose Mom and Dad, and meet my friends at the CD store. The Day After Thanksgiving Mad Dash is about to begin. You can do this, Britt. It's all in the timing. And we're looking...We're slowing down...There's a spot...We're parking...and ACTION!

"All right, hang on there just a minute, young lady."

(Screech!!) "Aw, Dad! Whaaat?"

"Brittany, don't talk to your father that way. This is a family outing, and we're all sticking together."

"Mother! You don't understand! They're releasing our totally favorite band's CD today! Do you know how many people are going to be waiting in line already?! Kayla and Vanessa even camped out. Their parents are cool."

I swear I had to have been adopted.

"Look, Brittany. I know you want to hang out with your friends to do your Christmas shopping. And that's fine. We've all got presents we want to buy. But, honestly, a little respect is all we're asking. We need to figure out a meeting place, set a time, and..."

Here we go again, acting like I'm two. I'm so sure, like I'm in the middle of line waiting to get my CD with ALL my friends, and I have to say, "Oh, sorry, guys. I have to meet my mommy and daddy!"

"Now, Brittany, if you're done rolling your eyes, we'll just meet at noon right here by the ChocoWorld candy store. Is that 'cool' enough for you?"

"Sure, fine, whatever. Gotta go!"

(Shouting from a distance) "Love you, Britt!"

(Hiding head in coat) *Oh, how embarrassing!*

Sound familiar? Sometimes parents make you want to hide your face until Jesus returns. But even Jesus had earthly parents who may have embarrassed him on occasion. Jesus knew that the way to honor his heavenly Father was to be obedient and respectful to his earthly parents. Maybe Jesus' parents didn't wear the coolest robes or this year's sandals. But they loved him, just as your parents love you. God has given our parents the authority to care for us, and by honoring them, we honor God...even if they can be embarrassing.

"Nobody's family can hang out the sign Nothing the Matter Here."
—CHINESE PROVERB

MY THOUGHTS:

"Honor your father and your mother, so that you may live long in the land the Lord your God is giving you."
—Exodus 20:12

MY PRAYERS:

Find a unique way to honor your family members, such as by blowing them away with the gift of time. Choose to stay home on a Friday night and have a family game night, or plan a thrifty fun day for a younger sibling. And remember, it will put a smile on God's face as well!

Unexpected Friendship

Consider this scenario: Jonathan, a prince of a very large nation, meets David, a shepherd.

What do they have in common? Nothing. What can they accomplish with nothing in common? Everything.

David might smell like a sour mixture of sheep dung, sweat, and blood (from wrestling a lion or two). He probably wears the same rags he calls clothes every day. Jonathan's father is the king. Jonathan probably has a fresh set of clothes each day. He lives in a palace of the nicest tents around—common housing back then. He may have a crown of gold, a royal robe, access to gold and armor...really anything he wants. He's even next in line for the throne! Right?

Well, not so much. In comes David and his dirty feet.

David and Jonathan were virtually opposites, with opposite talents, abilities, and backgrounds. One was a prince, the other a shepherd. One was rich, the other poor. One was in line for the throne, the other anointed for the throne. But their differences fused them together as best friends. They even made a covenant, promising to love each other as best friends for the rest of their lives.

God even wanted David, the poor, stinky shepherd, to become king. And Jonathan knew this guy was going to take his place on the throne. But they were still best friends, laying aside their differences and sticking together as close friends. More than once, Jonathan saved David's life and stuck up for his best friend when his father wanted David killed. Also more than once, David spared the life of his best friend's father—whom he could have easily killed—just because David made a promise to his best friend. That's loyalty.

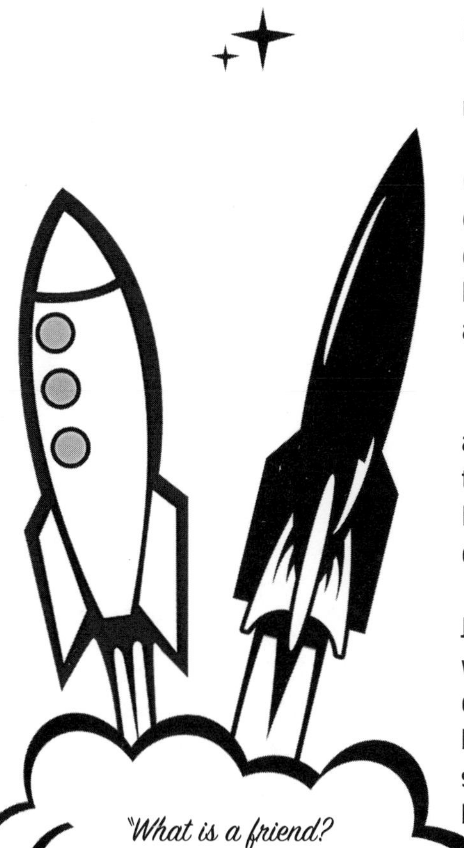

"What is a friend? A single soul dwelling in two bodies."
—ARISTOTLE

MY THOUGHTS:

"There are different kinds of gifts, but the same Spirit."
—1 Corinthians 12:4

DAILY Challenge™

Make a list of your character traits. Next to each one, write down one way you will use that trait to strengthen a friendship in your life.

MY PRAYERS:

So How Human Was Jesus?

Decide if each of the following statements is true or false.

1. Jesus was really God just "dressed up" as a human being.

2. Jesus was lucky he was God because he didn't really have to experience the pain of being human.

3. Jesus only had to experience temptation that one time in the desert.

4. Since Jesus was God, he didn't have to obey his parents.

5. Jesus knew everything—quantum mechanics, the theory of relativity, that I'd be here reading this now.

All these statements raise questions about the meaning of the Incarnation. The Incarnation is *the* paradox of Christianity—God becoming fully human while remaining fully God. One can think of it in terms of a novel. An author, while writing a novel, decides to write himself into the story. Now, the author's character in the book doesn't suddenly burst out of the pages into the face of the reader but works within the story and the world of the novel to change that world.

The author does not wear a "character suit"; he becomes a legitimate character (not just the voice of the author). Neither is Jesus just God in a "human suit." Because he was human, Jesus had to experience the emotional and physical pain of this world. Jesus wept after Lazarus' death, cried out in pain at his crucifixion, and ate after his resurrection. Jesus was tempted "in every way" (Hebrews 4:15), so we cannot assume that his temptations ended after his forty days in the desert. But because he was divine, Jesus never sinned.

Through both childhood and adulthood, Jesus was human. And through the Incarnation, God brought his kingdom to Earth.

"The result of the cosmic work of Christ is that the kingdom of God, God's rule over all things, is now manifest."
—ROBERT E. WEBBER

MY THOUGHTS:

"Who, being in very nature God, did not consider equality with God something to be grasped, but made himself nothing... being made in human likeness."
—Philippians 2:6-7

MY PRAYERS:

Talk to a child. Kneel down to be at the child's level. Avoid using adult vocabulary. Find out what he or she wants to talk about. See the world from the child's perspective. Love him or her the way a child needs to be loved. How is this like Jesus' incarnation?

"Change your opinions, keep to your principles; change your leaves, keep intact your roots."
–VICTOR HUGO

Surprise Birthday Party

Dear Diary,

This is NOT what the biology books told me. I know all about where babies come from, the stork and all, and there's no way Mother Mary got around Mother Nature. What am I supposed to do with a pregnant fiancée?!

I know what will happen. Even if we cover it up, elope, and then have the baby after we're married, my mom will be the first one to count back and realize it hasn't been a full nine months since the wedding. And then I'll get another lecture on responsibility or morality or, worse, on the birds and the bees. My mom will sit there and stare at that child to see whether it has my eyes.

And whose eyes will it have? I've been a righteous man, haven't messed around, have done everything I was supposed to. Mary tells me so sincerely that the child is a gift of God, not another man's, but what kind of story is that? I don't know if she's making it up or hallucinating; I've heard that pregnancy does strange things to a woman's hormones. But I thought they were supposed to crave pickles and figs, not imagine angels and virgin births.

Here's how the family photo album was supposed to go: new wife, good job, a few kids, no surprises. Here's how it's turning out: wife I can't keep, home I can't stay in, kid I don't recognize, and a big surprise birthday party.

And yet, angels say I should expect God's work in this. Perhaps this little boy will be more amazing than I can imagine. Perhaps he is to become a rabbi and lead the people. Of course, I can only guess—and pray.

Are you there, Lord? If so, could you please notice how much better the world would be if you wouldn't throw us curve balls like this? Please help me.

Joseph

OH, I KNOW IT SOUNDS CRAZY, MA... BUT YOU'VE JUST GOTTA BELIEVE ME!

MY THOUGHTS:

"His mother Mary was pledged to be married to Joseph, but before they came together, she was found to be with child through the Holy Spirit."
–Matthew 1:18

DAILY Challenge™

Take a walk somewhere familiar, but turn in a new direction and go somewhere you've never been before. Take time to think about the paths on which God has led you by surprise and how it made you feel.

MY PRAYERS:

Stay Close

"Not many TV characters have entered our living rooms and our hearts like 'Friends,' " wrote Marc Peyser in the article "Losing 'Friends,' " featured in a late 2003 issue of Newsweek magazine. Though *Friends* is gone from prime time, it probably won't be forgotten anytime soon.

When the TV show *Friends* debuted, there were no other shows like it on TV. For some reason, the chemistry between Chandler, Ross, Monica, Joey, Rachel, and Phoebe, and the people who play them, just worked. During the ten years *Friends* was on the air, the characters became close to many people. Viewers of the show began to get to know them and somehow feel like a part of their lives.

So what does this have to do with God? Well, you probably make a lot of decisions about what you want to do and who you want to do it with. No matter what your decisions are, one should be at the top of them all: Get to know Jesus. That doesn't mean you should read Bible history books, learn about different philosophical theories of God, or start learning Hebrew. Getting to know Jesus is very simple. You can spend time with him in prayer.

Prayer isn't just asking God for stuff and waiting for an answer. Think about it. *Friends* fans probably spent a half-hour at 8 p.m. every Thursday evening parked in front of their TVs. If they absolutely *had* to miss it, they taped it and watched it later. They'd watch reruns in the summer and maybe even watch the show in syndication on another channel.

Your actions reveal what's in your heart. Just as you'd spend a lot of time with a good friend, you'll spend a lot of time with Jesus if you want to be a closer "friend" with him. If you don't want to, start praying now that God will give you the desire.

So here's your challenge: Plot out a plan for spending time with Jesus in prayer. Get to know Jesus this year, and make him your very best friend.

"I become who I am as a Christian by relating to God. In ways mysterious and often hard to describe—yet never coercive or manipulative—I have changed over time because of my contact with God."

—PHILIP YANCEY

MY THOUGHTS:

"Like newborn babies, crave pure spiritual milk, so that by it you may grow up in your salvation, now that you have tasted that the Lord is good."
—1 Peter 2:2-3

MY PRAYERS:

Create a plan in your schedule for regular prayer time. Find a friend who wants to do the same thing, and share your goals with each other. Keep each other updated on how you're doing.

Odd Couples

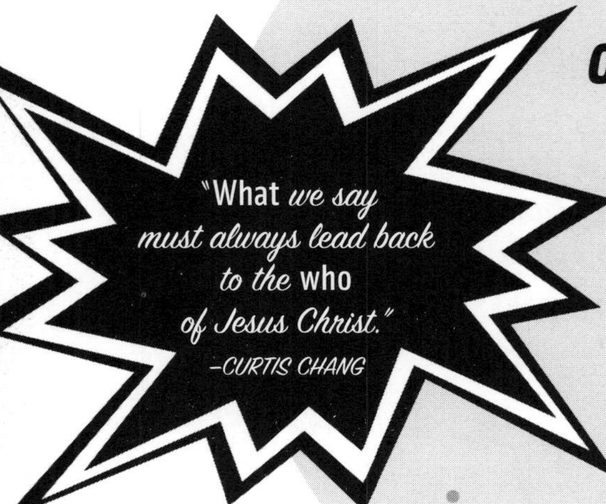

Can you complete each famous pair below?

- macaroni and ______________________
- vinegar and ______________________
- black and ______________________
- this and ______________________
- salt and ______________________
- Batman and ______________________
- Lewis and ______________________
- peanut butter and ______________________
- to and ______________________
- Romeo and ______________________
- socks and ______________________
- cats and ______________________

What do you think of this famous pair? Faith and science. Hold on a minute, many people would say. Faith and science don't go together! Or do they?

No matter what anyone believes, you have to start somewhere. Some choose to start with a belief in a scientific theory about the start of the universe and the formation of humans. However, as Christians, we start with a belief in a creative God, who with his own words created life. Both ways requires faith—either in a scientific phenomenon or in a personal God. So when it comes to beliefs about the creation of the world, even science uses faith!

By believing in God as the creative force behind all creation, we are able to better understand, experience, and explain the new creation that we each become when Jesus changes our lives. You see, since the very beginning of our universe, God has been interested in creation. He created the sky and the land. He created the sun and the stars. He created animals, birds, and fish. He created humans, and he created you. But that's not where it ends. When Jesus enters your life, he *re*-creates you, cleaning your soul and giving you a new start, and even now he is re-creating you to be more like him.

MY THOUGHTS:

____

____

____

____

____

"The earth is the Lord's, and everything in it, the world, and all who live in it."
—Psalm 24:1

MY PRAYERS:

____

____

____

____

____

Read part of a science textbook this week with "new eyes." Look at it not just as a report of scientific fact but as a record of the creative powers and unique design of the living God.

Two Kings

APRIL 4, 1968

We heard today that Martin Luther King Jr. was killed over in Memphis. He was giving a speech from his hotel room balcony, and some man shot him. I'm seventeen years old, way too old to cry in front of people like my little sister does all the time. But when they said he was dead, I burst into tears, surprising myself. I'm in my room now because being alone helps me figure out what's going on in my head. Actually, it's not as much my head as my heart, which feels as if it's been squeezed and pulled apart.

Almost five years ago in April of 1963, I was twelve, and my dad took me and my brother to see those people who were protesting the segregation of eating places in the city with sit-ins. I don't remember very much, except that all the demonstrators seemed so calm, peaceful, but determined—not violent or threatening, as so many people had said they were. I also have a perfect picture in my head of Martin Luther King Jr. as he sat during the protest and then as he was arrested with some others that same day. This sounds kind of dumb, and I'm almost embarrassed to say it, but I couldn't take my eyes off King the entire time because he...well, he shone. That's the best way I can put it. It was as if there was something in the air around him, and it made me want to meet him and find out what made him like that. My dad had told me he was a pastor and talked a lot about eternal life and a relationship with Jesus. I've wondered ever since what all that is about, but I never really knew what to think about God anyway, so I haven't done anything to find out.

But now he's dead, and I'm sad and hurt in a way I can't explain. But I also have so many questions, especially about the faith that this awesome man had—and lived his whole life by. Could I ever be like him? How can I find out about this relationship with God that he talked about, which made him light up from within and helped him impact the world?

"Injustice anywhere is a threat to justice everywhere. We are caught in an inescapable network of mutuality, tied in a single garment of destiny. Whatever affects one directly affects all indirectly."
—MARTIN LUTHER KING JR.

MY THOUGHTS:

"Be on your guard; stand firm in the faith; be men of courage; be strong. Do everything in love."
—1 Corinthians 16:13-14

Identify someone in your life who is treated unfairly or is the victim of prejudice. Be a loving advocate for him or her by giving the best gift of encouragement—your time. Invite this person over for dinner, and get to know him or her. Think of other ways you can live out God's love, and pray for justice in the lives of those around you.

MY PRAYERS:

"God's supervision is so blessedly true that at any given moment... whatever we may face we may say, 'For this cause came I unto this hour.'"
—JOHN STAM

It's the Little Things That Count

You sit in dark theaters (or perhaps living rooms) as Anakin Skywalker and Obi-Wan Kenobi dodge stars and fight with light sabers. You watch their adventures through three movies and hold your breath as they narrowly avoid death many times over. And yet, you aren't really that afraid for them because you know they will survive. You know the end of the story because it was possible to watch the sequels before the prequels ever came into existence. The end doesn't matter as much to you right now as do all the little details that lead up to the end. What exactly happens to make Anakin become Darth Vader? How were friendships made? Where did R2-D2 come from? How did the story unfold?

Now imagine what it would be like if you knew the end to every story ever told, if you knew how everything in the world ends. Well, God does. And while you may not know everything *he* does, you do know the big-picture ending—that God wins by defeating evil, and everyone who has a relationship with Jesus gets to live with him forever! And because you already know the end of the story, you can concentrate on the details in your story that lead up to that end. In his book *The Sacred Romance,* John Eldredge relates what his wife said about knowing the end of a story: "It only takes away the fear and frees you to enjoy the drama." Every day, you can enjoy the drama as God leads you through life, pleased with and glorified by the details of your amazing story!

MY THOUGHTS:

"My eyes will watch over them for their good...I will build them up and not tear them down; I will plant them and not uproot them. I will give them a heart to know me, that I am the Lord. They will be my people, and I will be their God, for they will return to me with all their heart."
—Jeremiah 24:6-7

MY PRAYERS:

DAILY Challenge™

Write the ending of a story, then write the rest of the story. Do the characters seem different to you than they would have if you had started from the beginning? What about the plot? How important are the details since you already know the structure of the story? Thank God that he knows the ending to your story, and ask him to help you live out the details in a way that glorifies him.

Following the Leader

> *"What other people think of me is becoming less and less important; what they think of Jesus because of me is critical."*
> —CLIFF RICHARDS

Instructor: All right, Ms. Hearter. Are we ready to begin your driving lesson?

MH: Ready as always! Seatbelt fastened...hands at ten and two... break left, gas...RIGHT THERE IN FRONT OF US—IT'S A JESUS FISH!

Instructor: A what?

MH: A Jesus fish on the back of that car! Hold on! *(She peels out of parking lot after the "Jesus fish" car, wheels squealing.)*

Instructor: Ms. Hearter, this is nuts! What are you doing?

MH: Sorry! I just can't help it! It's as if the fish has some magnetic pull over me! Must follow fish!

Instructor: Ms. Hearter, the curb! Look out for that *(crash)* mailbox! Oh, great—that's gotta be illegal. We're pulling government property...

MH: Must follow fish! Makes me want to sing! I'll just roll down the windows and shout, "Jesus, Jesus, Jesus!"

Instructor: *(Screaming)* Get your head back in the window! And get back in your lane!

MH: Say, did I ever tell you about a friend I know? His name is Jesus! And he's my very best friend in the whole wide world. And that's his fish we're followin'!

Instructor: Ms. Hearter, do you realize how many laws you've broken since we pulled out of the school? All just for following this "fish"! Oh no...slow down! The fish is getting closer; they're putting on their BRAKES!!! *(Crash)*

As Christians we're called to follow Christ, but it's important to be aware of *how* we're following. When we first become Christians, it's easy to become so fired up that we reel out of control, "driving" recklessly. While proclaiming Jesus' name, we can break rules and mow down non-Christians with our enthusiasm if we're not careful. Take note of how you come across to others, especially those who don't know Jesus. By spending time in God's Word, you will get a clear glimpse of who Jesus is, what he did, and the things he said, which will help you know how to model the one you're following.

MY THOUGHTS:

"But you will receive power when the Holy Spirit comes on you; and you will be my witnesses in Jerusalem, and in all Judea and Samaria, and to the ends of the earth."
—Acts 1:8

MY PRAYERS:

Ask God to reveal one area of your life that needs special attention in the way you're portraying him to others. Develop a game plan to tackle that area, and consider the choices you'll make the next time you are faced with a chance to share Jesus with others. Pray for the Holy Spirit to guide you.

"In a sense, of course, all believers are strangers in a strange land—some, as they say, are just stranger than others."
—MARCIA FORD

Messages From God

God has been talking to me again, telling me to do strange things. I think today's command is the weirdest yet, stranger than eating the scroll, stranger than making that model of Jerusalem under siege. God tells me to do things that are totally abnormal but also pretty extraordinary. People certainly pay attention because what God tells me to do is so dramatic!

This time, so the people know their beloved city of Jerusalem will be under siege because of their sin, God told me to lie on my left side for 390 days as a way of bearing the sins of Israel upon myself. After that, I'm supposed to turn over and bear the sin of Judah on my right side for forty days. God said he will tie me up with ropes so that I cannot turn from one side to the other until I have finished. Thankfully, God did say I could eat. He said to get a storage jar and put wheat, barley, beans, lentils, millet and spelt into it. God said to make bread from this, as I would make a barley cake. (Though how will I cook while I'm tied up?) I am also allowed two-thirds of a quart of water each day.

The idea of our wonderful city under siege and people starving makes me very sad. But I trust God and will obey him because I know he doesn't always communicate with his people through subtle means or totally "normal" people! And normal is one thing I'm not...

(Read more about Ezekiel's story in Ezekiel 4:4-17!)

MY THOUGHTS:

"The people to whom I am sending you are obstinate and stubborn. Say to them, 'This is what the Sovereign Lord says.'"
—Ezekiel 2:4

DAILY Challenge™

Talk to other Christians. Has God ever asked them to do something weird? What strange behavior, commanded by God, is recorded in the Scriptures? What does this tell you about God, and how can you apply it to your life?

MY PRAYERS:

Dating the Best Way

Before your next date, take a look at this list of dating do's and don'ts.

- **Do** take a cotton swab in case of a horrifying ear-wax emergency, but...
- **Don't** clean your ears in front of your date.
- **Do** teach your dog a new trick to impress your date, but...
- **Don't** smooch the dog in front of your date (dog breath—need I say more?).
- **Do** make sure your shoes match, but...
- **Don't** forget the odor-eaters.
- **Do** take a cell phone for emergencies, but
- **Don't** play those cell-phone games during your date unless you're really good at them.

Though she wasn't talking about dating, the quote on this page by Katie Couric could apply to it. You've got a lot of choices, which can either be great or overwhelming. But as you make choices in your dating life, remember that prayer can change everything, so make prayer a priority in your dating experience. And if you want to have a good date, pray before your date. No kidding. It will make a huge difference!

If you want an example from the Bible of a really cool, God-focused romance, check out Jacob and Rachel in Genesis 29:1-28. Jacob was so in love with Rachel that he worked for her father, Laban, for fourteen years so he could marry her. The first seven years "seemed like only a few days to him because of his love for her" (Genesis 29:20b). Aw, that's sweet.

Now go have a great date!

*"The good news is,
you have a lot of choices,
and the bad news is,
you have a lot of choices."*
—KATIE COURIC

THOUGHTS:

"Trust in the Lord with all your heart and lean not on your own understanding; in all your ways acknowledge him, and he will make your paths straight."
—Proverbs 3:5-6

PRAYERS:

DAILY Challenge™

Go ask your parents about their dating experiences when they were your age. Get a piece of paper and markers, and create a list of do's and don'ts for dating based on what you think would make God and your parents proud. Post the list somewhere in your room so it will be a reminder to always make good dating choices.

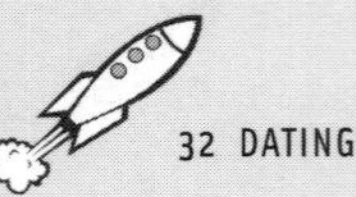

God's GPS

Jeremy: Uh, Alan? We've been driving around for three hours now, and I think we've passed that tree several hundred times.

Alan: Oh, don't be ridiculous...maybe *one* hundred.

Jeremy: Come on, man. Let's stop and ask for directions or something. I can't believe you forgot your cell!

Alan: Well, you're the one who was supposed to bring the map in the first place.

Jeremy: I know! I'll leave a trail out the window using crumbs from all the Pop-Tarts we brought.
Then we can figure out where we've been at least.

Alan: No good.

Jeremy: Why's that?

Alan: Ate 'em.

Jeremy: All of them?!

Alan: Yup.

Jeremy: Great. So we're lost—no map, no cell phone, no food.

Alan: Yeah, what a joke. Say, would you see if you could at least get this funky stereo system working?
It keeps lighting up with these weird lines every time I try.

Jeremy: Alan! It's a GPS!

Alan: Yeah, I know—a great big piece-of-junk stereo.

Jeremy: No, ya big goof! A Global Positioning System. This device lets us know where we are! All we have to do is plug in the info. It will help us get back on track and stay on track so we can get where we need to be!

Alan: Wow! Good thing I had you with me, man. So since we don't have the Pop-Tarts, we'll just take out this GPS and leave it here. Then we'll know if we've been this way before and...

Jeremy: I'm so glad you aren't alone.

We can be glad that we aren't alone, either. God has set up a GPS for us in our relationship with him. Wherever you are, whether you feel lost or have strayed off the path, or maybe are just cruisin' right along, take time to let God know. Let him be your guide, and know that he will always lead you in the right direction. A great way to make sure you're staying on course is to find an accountability partner, a trusted person who you know will encourage you in your faith. A weekly check-in from someone who is praying for you can make all the difference in the world, and it will let you know that you aren't going through life alone.

MY THOUGHTS:

"A friend is one who makes me do my best."
—OSWALD CHAMBERS

"But if the watchman sees the sword coming and does not blow the trumpet to warn the people and the sword comes and takes the life of one of them, that man will be taken away because of his sin, but I will hold the watchman accountable for his blood."
—Ezekiel 33:6

Find an accountability partner, and set a time and place to check in each week to share struggles, seek guidance, and pray for help to keep on the straight and narrow path!

Can You Hear Me Now?

"God shapes the world by prayer."
–E.M. BOUNDS

It is hard for many of us to imagine life without a cell phone. Almost no one remembers having to hunt all over town to find a pay phone just to call for directions. And yet, with all our technology, we still find ourselves saying into our cell phones, "Can you hear me? Can you hear me?"

Often, when we try to talk to God, we feel as if he is not hearing us. We pray and pray, and then we stop and ask, "Can you hear me?" Sometimes the problems we have with prayer are not unlike those we have with our cell phones.

• Out of range: We pray for God to do things for us, but we don't realize that our relationships with God are way out of shape. Before we ask for God to do stuff for us, we need to make sure our lives are right with him.

• Low battery: Prayer is often the last thing we do at night or the first thing we do in the morning. However, if we don't plan our lives well, we find that we are too sleepy and tired for prayer to be truly effective. Leave both time and energy in your life to pray!

• No signal: Sometimes we give up praying when we feel that God is not answering. However, we must persist. It is often in this persistence that we learn faith, wisdom, and hope.

So keep praying. He can hear you. He can hear you now.

MY THOUGHTS:

"Pray continually."
–1 Thessalonians 5:17

MY PRAYERS:

DAILY Challenge™

Keep a prayer journal. In it, mark the date and time you prayed as well as what you prayed for. Leave space to go back and mark how and when the prayers were answered.

How to Know More Than You Thought You Did

I never knew that!

What are the colors of the spectrum in order? It may be difficult to remember red, orange, yellow, green, blue, indigo, and violet. It's much easier when you take the first letters of each color and spell an imaginary name: Roy G. Biv.

In music, what are the notes of the treble clef? It's easy to remember "F-A-C-E" for the spaces, and once you learn it, "Every Good Boy Deserves Fudge" is something you'll remember for the line notes even when you're old.

Who could forget "Columbus sailed the ocean blue in 1492" or "*i* before *e* except after *c* or when sounding like *a,* as in neighbor and weigh"?

Mnemonic devices like these use rhymes, phrases, or other techniques to make remembering information easier. Most people create their own when preparing for tests. Mnemonics make us more likely to remember what we've studied.

Thankfully, the Holy Spirit is more powerful and effective than any mnemonic. He's not a parlor trick or study aid to help you ace geometry or science class. What he does is far more important! Jesus told his disciples that the Holy Spirit would teach them things and help them remember everything Jesus taught them. And he'll do the same for us. As we study and read God's Word, the Holy Spirit helps us remember and apply those truths to every situation we face.

Feeling anxious? The Holy Spirit can remind you of God's power and presence. Don't know if something is right or wrong? The Holy Spirit will nudge you in the right direction, often bringing Bible verses to your mind at just the right time.

Just as mnemonics only work if you take time to learn them, you must spend time in God's Word and prayer. Ask the Holy Spirit to speak to you. Ask him to lead and teach you. Then, when you're tested and need answers, ask the Holy Spirit to remind you of God's truth. With his help, you'll pass life's test with high marks.

"When the Spirit illuminates the heart, then a part of the man sees which never saw before; a part of him knows which never knew before."
—A. W. TOZER

MY THOUGHTS:

"The Holy Spirit, whom the Father will send in my name, will teach you all things and will remind you of everything I have said to you."
—John 14:26

Read a portion of the Bible. Really pay attention. Ask the Holy Spirit to teach you through your reading and to bring what God has said in his Word to your memory—right when you need it.

MY PRAYERS:

Multiple-Choice Service

Dear Mayor Malone,

How can a student like me make a difference for the poor in our city? I've tried giving out spare change, but I can't tell if that really does anything. And my dad says I shouldn't give anything because they'll just spend it on alcohol. I feel so guilty when I just walk past a homeless person on the street, and I want to do something that really makes a difference. Plus, since I'm a Christian, I think it's what Jesus would want me to do. Please help me to help!

Sincerely,

Charity Pennywise

OFFICIAL MEMO

Dear Charity,

Great question! Let me show you a menu of different ways to feed the needy, and you can try the ones that work best for you and your neighborhood.

- Have a parent or pastor go with you to take a homeless person out to lunch. Take time to actually get to know them—we all need love a lot more than spare change.
- Volunteer with a local food pantry or shelter. Every student should experience this before they graduate from high school. Interview one of the staff workers at the pantry about how they make a real difference for the poor.
- Write to your congressional representatives, and tell them that, as an up-and-coming voter, you're going to vote for the candidates who can do the most for the poor. We really read those letters!
- Volunteer with a meal-service program that delivers food to the homes of those who need it. Sometimes poor people are not homeless but could really use some extra help.
- Tutor a child in the inner city. Sometimes the best thing you can do to help the poor is prevent future problems. Helping a kid have a better life now will have a huge impact on him or her later on.
- Remember that the Bible says God wants you to be motivated by love; it doesn't say that God wants you to be motivated by guilt.

Hope that helps you help someone! Write me back, and let me know what happens!

Sincerely,

Mayor Malone

Serve Others

"The trouble is that rich people... very often don't really know who the poor are; and that is why we can forgive them."
—MOTHER TERESA

MY THOUGHTS:

"All they asked was that we should continue to remember the poor, the very thing I was eager to do." —Galatians 2:10

Do something to serve the poor. Whatever you choose to do, do it with the purpose of loving others and learning what it means to be a servant. If you're uncomfortable doing it, ask God to help you see with his eyes.

MY PRAYERS:

Career Detour

> *"'I will take the Ring,' he said, 'though I do not know the way.'"*
> –*FRODO IN* THE FELLOWSHIP OF THE RING *BY J.R.R. TOLKIEN*

Even as a child, Jess wondered what she would do for a career. She discovered in high school that she had many talents, and although she often prayed that God would show her the way, she was impatient for the answer. It just seemed like all her friends already knew what they wanted to do for a living.

In college, Jess was required to participate in a community-service project. She chose to volunteer at a homeless shelter, and during her time there, she reorganized the shelter and helped them add programs and receive more funding. Jess loved working there and had a great time playing with the children. But when the owner begged her to come and run the shelter after she graduated, she turned him down without praying about it. She didn't consider a homeless-shelter director to be among the types of careers in her future, and she reasoned that her talents would qualify her for many different opportunities.

She was right. She graduated from the university at the top of her class and interviewed for many types of great jobs. Seeking the perfect career, she went on many trips to interview with companies all over the country. She knew that, on one of these trips, she would find the job God wanted her to have.

She was right again. While waiting outside the airport to get a ride to an interview, a homeless boy approached her for money. Since they were in her college city, Jess told the boy to go to the homeless shelter where she had volunteered. The boy told her dejectedly that he had been there only one time...before it closed. Jess couldn't believe it. She hailed a taxi, and instead of going to her interview, she went to the shelter with the boy. He was right—it was closed. A sign said the shelter had run out of funding. Jess didn't know what to do but decided to pray that God would show her the way. Then she knocked on the shelter door. The owner who had once asked Jess to run the shelter came to the door. The owner smiled and said, "I knew God would lead you back to us."

Jess looked at the owner and the little boy and realized the truth. On this trip, God *had* shown her what job he wanted her to have.

With a map, plan a vacation path of your choice. How would you get to your destination? What are some detours that might alter your path? With a Bible, plan a possible career path of God's choice. Considering the career, answer the questions again.

MY THOUGHTS:

"Let nothing move you. Always give yourselves fully to the work of the Lord, because you know that your labor in the Lord is not in vain." —1 Corinthians 15:58

MY PRAYERS:

"We talk of loving others for who they are inside, not understanding that to really love we must love the whole person, including the body."
—LILIAN CALLES BARGER

Rebellious Images

Did you know?

• The average Miss America contestant works out fourteen hours a week (and some up to thirty-five!).

• Of girls in the first to third grades, 42 percent want to be thinner.

• In America, more than eight million people suffer from eating disorders, including anorexia nervosa and bulimia. Women make up 90 percent of the cases.

• In the United States, there were six times as many face-lifts in 1999 as there were in 1990.

How do you respond when you hear statistics like these? This is probably not the first time you've thought about the dissatisfaction people in our society have with their bodies. Maybe you don't like certain things about the way you look. Maybe you think that if you looked better, more guys or girls would like you, you'd be more popular, and you'd have some control.

Scripture teaches that God created people in his image. What does this mean? Think about a great artist who decides to paint a self-portrait. He uses the finest paints and canvas and takes his time to make the most beautiful piece of art ever. Then, the artist brings the portrait to life. The portrait should feel honored, shouldn't it? It is inspired by and has received life from the greatest artist in the world! But sadly, the portrait hates itself, complains about the colors, and dislikes the fine canvas. The painting rejects itself and its maker.

As humans created by God in his image, our whole being—our emotions, intellect, reason, creative capacity, relational desires, and physical body—reflects who he is. Paradoxically, though, we possess a sinful nature that wants to ruin the image of God in us. One way we mar God's image is by hating our outward appearance and disliking what God has created. Instead, we need to accept our whole selves as God's image and be thankful for his creation—us.

MY THOUGHTS:

____

____

____

____

____

Look through a magazine with critical eyes. Which advertisements are designed to make you dislike your appearance and achieve "satisfaction" by purchasing beauty or image products? Try to spend a length of time away from things that make you dissatisfied with yourself. How do you feel then?

"So God created man in his own image, in the image of God he created him; male and female he created them."
—Genesis 1:27

MY PRAYERS:

____

____

____

____

____

Why It's Good to Be a Clown

Michael Christensen is a clown. And he's real proud of it. He and Paul Binder are co-founders of the Big Apple Circus, created in 1977 and now "one of the most beloved institutions in New York City, with a 1,700-seat big-top tent, more than 500,000 visitors each year, and numerous community outreach programs" (Biography magazine, April 2003).

One of those programs is called the Clown Care Unit. It began when Christensen brought a few of his circus friends to a special event at Columbia Presbyterian Medical Center. He loved entertaining the children in the hospital, and the Clown Care Unit was soon launched. Christensen (a.k.a. "Dr. Stubs") and his clown friends give their time and talents to help bring smiles to the faces of very sick children. They love doing it, and the kids love it too.

But it's not without difficult moments. Christensen recalls a time when two clowns entered a room in the Intensive Care Unit at Schneider Children's Hospital in Queens, New York. They saw people standing around a bed saying nothing and decided it might be best to leave them alone. However, a nurse brought them back in, explaining that a baby had just died and the mother wanted them to play some music. So with their flute and concertina, the two clowns played while the mother sat in a rocking chair with the baby. When the clowns told Christensen about the sad moment with tears in their eyes, he told them, "Usually angels are delegated to do this work. You did it instead."

We do things every day for different reasons. But for whom do we do them? For others? For our parents? For ourselves? God wants you to do everything as if you are working for him. No matter what you do, do it with him in mind. You never know what lives he'll change through your work, and he will never forget it.

(Source: "Rx for Sick Kids: Send in the Clowns!" by Laurie Sandell, Biography magazine, April 2003)

> *"If you're going to care about the fall of the sparrow you can't pick and choose who's going to be the sparrow. It's everybody."*
>
> *—ADAM IN*
> THE ARM OF THE STARFISH
> *BY MADELEINE L'ENGLE*

MY THOUGHTS:

"Whatever you did for one of the least of these brothers of mine, you did for me."
—Matthew 25:40

MY PRAYERS:

Look through a photo album, and find a picture of one person who impacted your life in a positive way or encouraged you. Pray for that person, and think of one way you can return the favor to that person or someone else.

Three Days, Two Voices

Voice One—the Cross

They thrust me toward the criminal's shoulder, and he fell down with my weight, so they grabbed another guy and made him carry me. We went to The Place of the Skull, which is where all the crosses go to be used. They laid me down there, pushed him on top of me, tied his arms to my crossbeam, and nailed his ankles and wrists to me. Then they hoisted us up and stuck me into the ground. I could hear him trying to breathe as they nailed a sign over his head that said "The King of the Jews." I had never heard of a king being crucified before, and I wondered what he had done to merit crucifixion. People are usually more respectful of kings. Bystanders walked past us, insulting the king by saying, "You who are going to destroy the temple and build it in three days, save yourself! Come down from the cross, if you are the Son of God!" Others said, "He's the King of Israel! Let him come down now from the cross, and we will believe in him." But whoever he was—king or Son of God—he didn't leave. He continued to breathe for about three hours, and then he died.

(Story from Matthew 27:32-50.)

Voice Two—the Woman

It was the day after the Sabbath, and I was glad to visit Jesus' tomb. But when I got there, the boulder had been moved. I was so surprised and sad that I stood and wept in the garden. Suddenly, from inside the tomb, a voice said, "Woman, why are you crying?" There were two angels in the tomb! I was shocked but answered truthfully, "They have taken my Lord away, and I don't know where they put him." Before they had a chance to answer, I turned around and saw a man who also asked me why I was crying. I thought he was the gardener and might know where Jesus' body was. "If you have carried him away, tell me where you have put him, and I will get him," I said. Then the gardener said "Mary," and I recognized him as Jesus! I have seen the Lord! He is risen from the grave!

(Story from John 20:1-18.)

"For Jesus we have taken this cross; for Jesus let us persevere. He will be our help, Who is our guide and leader."

—THOMAS á KEMPIS

MY THOUGHTS:

"He himself bore our sins in his body on the tree, so that we might die to sins and live for righteousness; by his wounds you have been healed."

—1 Peter 2:24

Remember the story of Jesus' passion by praying in the dark with only one candle lit. Thank God for Jesus' incarnation, birth, and death. Then turn on the light, and praise God for the resurrection of Jesus. Hallelujah! He is risen!

MY PRAYERS:

The Loners

Meet the Loner family. Jimmy Loner rarely sees his parents or his sister, Sally Loner. Sometimes they pass in the hall or maybe have a quick meal together, but that doesn't happen very often. Mr. Loner leaves for work at 6:30 a.m. every day, long before the rest of the Loners get up. Sally leaves for school before Jimmy is out of the shower, and Mom Loner only gets a chance to talk with Jimmy on the way to the bus stop.

In the evenings, Jimmy has soccer and Sally has ballet (though Jimmy doesn't really know what kind of dance class Sally is in). Dad picks up the kids but once forgot to pick up Sally. It worked out because Sally got a ride with her best friend, Mindy. Mom goes to bed early, Jimmy stays up late with homework, and Dad likes to work on his building projects. Don't worry about the Loners, though; they see each other every day.

The poor Loner family. Their lives are filled with so many activities that they never really get to spend time together. Sure, they may pass each other going in and out, but they never really connect, so it becomes nearly impossible for them to grow as a family. This is easy to see.

What is not so easy to see is that the same can be true with the family of Christians. If we never go to church or Bible study or youth group, we end up losing touch with our Christian family. (The Bible calls fellow Christians "brothers and sisters" for a reason!) And fellowship with other Christians has some serious perks: encouragement, friendship, laughter, spiritual support, learning, and growth. Being Loner Christians means we miss out on the great benefits of being with people who have relationships with Jesus. When we prioritize building relationships with others, we will find ourselves connected with one another and with God.

"[The church is] something that God has brought into being, something that is worthy and valuable, something that is going to last forever."
—A.W. TOZER

HEY, LOOK... THERE'S A WEDNESDAY NIGHT WORSHIP SERVICE AT CHURCH—LET'S GO!!!

MY THOUGHTS:

"Let us not give up meeting together."
—Hebrews 10:25a

MY PRAYERS:

DAILY Challenge™

Go to a worship service, or, if worship is already a habit, go to an event at church you don't usually attend, like prayer meeting or evening service.

True Enough

Ever wonder how Christianity stacks up next to the other world religions? With all the faiths out there, how can anyone say Christianity is correct? In a court of law, what would be the evidence for Christianity? Of course, a transforming relationship with Jesus cannot be proved, tested, and measured in the same way other things are, but take a moment to think through this "evidence."

• Historical data: Ancient Jewish historian Josephus and Roman historian Tacitus both record that Jesus actually lived.

• Archaeology: Archaeological digs have discovered bits of evidence that support the stories of the Bible, including the tomb of James, Jesus' brother; the pool of Bethesda; and the tomb of Caiaphas, the high priest.

• Silence: No non-Christian has been able to develop a satisfactory explanation of how the story of Jesus' resurrection spread throughout the world within a few decades.

• Eyewitness accounts: Several different people who either knew Jesus personally or knew his friends personally wrote accounts of his life. Remember, the Bible wasn't originally one book; it was several books from different sources who all told the same story.

• Experience: Christians all over the world experience answered prayer, miracles, and the power of Jesus in their lives. Literally millions of personal experiences would have to be dismissed to prove Christianity false.

• Forensics: The tombs of every major religious leader from the past are occupied...except one.

MY THOUGHTS:

"Always be prepared to give an answer to everyone who asks you to give the reason for the hope that you have."
—1 Peter 3:15

MY PRAYERS:

Research another religion, and find out exactly how it is different from Christianity. You could read about it, watch an informational video, or talk to a person of another faith. Find out about the needs that only Jesus can meet.

Extra! Extra! Read All About It!

If there had been newspapers in the city of Jericho during this period, these would have been the headlines. Even without newspapers, the people of Jordan had heard that the Israelites were coming and that their God was giving them great power.

Rahab told the Israelite spies that the hearts of her people had melted in fear and their courage was gone. Yet none but Rahab turned and acknowledged the God of the Israelites. None but Rahab realized that the power of this foreign God was not only awesome, it was ultimate. Only Rahab saw more than an enemy in those headlines. She saw a God who was powerful, yes, but she also saw a God who was faithful and devoted to his people, a God who would protect and love those people. And she saw a people who been given a vision and a purpose.

Rahab heard, and she believed. She recognized God in the headlines and changed her life. She followed God and the Israelites, and she became the great-great-grandmother of King David.

Have you heard or seen the presence of God in those around you? Have you noticed God moving and working in the world? If so, have you, like Rahab, acknowledged God's power in those moments? Or have you, like the people of Jericho, ignored the reality of God's movement? God is alive and working all around you. He is still performing miracles, still providing for his people, and still changing lives. It is up to us to notice God in the daily grind, and it is up to us to acknowledge his presence and power in our own lives. The more we do, the more we will understand how amazing life is when we serve such a God. (To read more about Rahab, check out Joshua 2 and 6!)

"The presence of God became unutterably real and blessed... For what service I was accepted I knew not, but a deep consciousness that I was not my own took possession of me."
—HUDSON TAYLOR

MY THOUGHTS:

"We have heard how the Lord dried up the water of the Red Sea for you when you came out of Egypt, and what you did to Sihon and Og, the two kings of the Amorites east of the Jordan, whom you completely destroyed. When we heard of it, our hearts melted and everyone's courage failed because of you, for the Lord your God is God in heaven above and on the earth below."
—Joshua 2:10-11

Do some "God-spotting" this week. Look for God in those around you. Make a note or card for each person you see God working through, and thank those people for allowing God to use their lives as witnesses of his power and love.

MY PRAYERS:

"No man can break any of the Ten Commandments. He can only break himself against them."
—G. K. CHESTERTON

Out of Love and Obedience

You've heard lots of good reasons not to drink alcohol or take mind-altering drugs—they harm your body, affect your mind, support crime and terrorism, and lead to tragedy and heartache.

What's the best reason you've ever heard (or given) for not drinking or doing drugs? Where does "My parents won't let me" rank on your list of really good reasons not to drink or take drugs?

Evidently, God thought it was a pretty good one. God sent the prophet Jeremiah to visit Jaazaniah and his Recabite family and offer them wine. When Jeremiah set the wine before them and offered it to them, the Recabites didn't worry about whether it was socially acceptable to refuse a drink. They didn't worry that someone might think they needed to grow up and think for themselves.

Many generations earlier, an ancestor, Jonadab, had told his children never to drink wine and to pass on the order to following generations. Jaazaniah and all his brothers, sisters, and relatives were just the latest generation of Recabites to honor those wishes with wholehearted respect and obedience. God publicly commended the Recabites and promised to bless them for their faithful obedience.

God wants us to honor our parents, our elders, and those in authority over us. Such obedience and respect brings glory and ultimate obedience to him. So even if you don't see anything wrong with taking a drink of alcohol now and then or using drugs, it would be disregarding God's Word for you to disobey your parents or elders in the Lord who don't want you to.

And it goes beyond that. Even if your parents are permissive about drugs and alcohol, or even if they use drugs or alcohol themselves, it still doesn't make it OK for you. Argue all you want about what the Bible says or doesn't say. For you, it doesn't matter. Abstaining from alcohol isn't just a good idea: For people under a certain age, it's the law. And using illegal drugs or misusing prescription drugs is never OK—not for anyone. So honor God and those in authority above you. Just say no!

MY THOUGHTS:

"We do not drink wine, because our forefather Jonadab son of Recab gave us this command: 'Neither you nor your descendants must ever drink wine.' "
—Jeremiah 35:6

MY PRAYERS:

DAILY Challenge™

Discuss the issue of drugs and alcohol with your parents or a trusted Christian adult. What are their views and concerns? What are the dangers of alcohol or drugs? How can you honor their wishes for you and obey the laws against drugs and alcohol?

Bible Camp S.O.S.

Dear Mom,

I really need your help. I'm supposed to share my "faith story" on Friday night at the campfire. I'm already scared. See, every night here at camp, we have a fire. Someone tells about what God has done in their lives, how they got to know Jesus, and so on. Some of these people have great stories! One guy told about how he used to be totally mean and beat kids up, and then he learned about how Jesus treated weak people, and so he quit. Another girl told about how she had two abortions before she began a relationship with Jesus and learned about the way God loves her...and values other human life. Can you see why I'm scared? I don't have anything dramatic or exciting to share! I mean, you and Dad taught me about God and Jesus from before I can remember, and I've always believed. Do you have any advice to make my boring story more interesting?

Love, Kerry

"Every night I was on my knees—and nothing happened. I didn't feel purged of sin or close to the Lord. I didn't feel what some of the others felt so sincerely."
—ETHEL WATERS

Dear Kerry,

It was good to hear from you! I can understand your apprehension as you prepare for Friday night. Those stories are certainly a hard act to follow! But do you know what? Faith stories are not an act! Though others' stories might be more dramatic, God's hand is just as evident in your life. Remember last year when you had so many doubts about everything in Christianity? We prayed together, and then you (I love this about you!) started reading your way through our church library—all those theology books and commentaries! Though I'm not sure if all your questions were answered (Are they ever?), this was an important part of your journey to where you are now.

Don't think of this as your moment in the spotlight, Kerry. Think of this as God's story in the spotlight. Hope this helps! Blessings for Friday, Kerry.

I love you, Mom

MY THOUGHTS:

"Just as you received Christ Jesus as Lord, continue to live in him, rooted and built up in him, strengthened in the faith as you were taught, and overflowing with thankfulness."
—Colossians 2:6-7

MY PRAYERS:

DAILY Challenge™

There are many opportunities to tell your faith story. Each one requires a different way of telling. Jot down ideas about how to tell your story to a group of Christians at camp, a non-Christian friend, and a small group of Christians and non-Christians at school.

Biker Followers

> *"If I die, I want to write on the wall with my blood, 'Jesus is alive.'"*
>
> —LALANI JAYASINGHE, A CHRISTIAN IN SRI LANKA WHO SUFFERED PERSECUTION, DEATH THREATS, AND HER HUSBAND'S MURDER AS A RESULT OF THEIR CHRISTIAN BELIEFS

There's a motorcycle gang in Indiana called the Unchained Gang. Sure, some of the members have a "checkered" past, and some of them may look a little rough or scary, but they're not dangerous. They're Christians.

In his book *Riders for God,* Rich Remsberg says, "Made up primarily of former bikers and drug dealers, ex-convicts and recovering addicts, the Unchained Gang is an outreach ministry, going into Indiana prisons and jails, biker rallies, and other places where people on the fringe are ignored by other churches and the rest of society." Here are profiles of two members of this influential gang.

Pastor Larry has been the president of the Unchained Gang for many years and is the pastor of the House of Prayer, where most of the gang members attend church. He's not formally trained as a minister. His life before the Unchained Gang involved drugs, alcohol, and "outlaw motorcycle clubs," among other things. He became a Christian in 1978.

Randy is a deacon at the House of Prayer. He first went to jail when he was eleven. He also attended reform schools and was sent to a few different foster homes. His dad was an alcoholic. After reform school, Randy found it hard to fit back into life somewhere, so he settled into a life of drugs, alcohol, and living on the streets. He's been arrested a lot...maybe 200 times or more. He spent three years in Alcoholics Anonymous before he became a Christian.

Members of the Unchained Gang now spend their time telling others their stories and introducing people to Jesus. And what powerful stories they have! But anyone who's experienced the changing power of God's love can make a difference like the members of the Unchained Gang. You don't have to have a "checkered past," and you also don't have to be a minister or an expert on the Bible. Don't let the thought of telling someone about Jesus' love be an intimidating one. You already have everything you need to pass on his message of love: a relationship with Jesus himself!

MY THOUGHTS:

"Through love and faithfulness sin is atoned for; through the fear of the Lord a man avoids evil." —Proverbs 16:6

MY PRAYERS:

For one day, take a notebook with you wherever you go, and write down every instance of God revealing his love for you. Write everything down, no matter how small it seems.

Retired Man Saves Raspberries

At the Los Angeles Wholesale Produce Market in 1987, Mickey Weiss watched in horror as 200 flats of ripe raspberries made their way to the dumpster to be crushed with the rest of the day's trash. A retired produce wholesaler, Weiss understood the value of the fresh fruit. He also knew there were many hungry people in Southern California that the red berries could feed.

Weiss quickly chose to come out of retirement and began working out of donated office space. He called food banks, kitchens, and produce wholesalers and asked all of them to use good food in a way that would serve the community. Eventually, he formed a team of volunteers from the Los Angeles Wholesale Produce Market and the L.A. County Department of Agriculture.

The result of the raspberry dream? Weiss' Charitable Distribution Facility now serves Southern California by distributing more than 2 million pounds of fresh produce to help low-income families each month.

A nationwide effort was established in 1991 to help low-income Americans everywhere eat fresh produce. From the Wholesaler to the Hungry, which helps other cities create projects similar to the Charitable Distribution Facility, is making it happen—all because one man dreamed of saving some raspberries... and helping millions.

(Source: U.S. Department of Agriculture)

MY THOUGHTS:

"Everybody talks about the weather, but nobody does anything about it."
—MARK TWAIN

"Therefore, I urge you, brothers, in view of God's mercy, to offer your bodies as living sacrifices, holy and pleasing to God—this is your spiritual act of worship."
—Romans 12:1

Sometime during the week, ask a friend, a teacher, and a family member to each tell you the greatest thing they have ever done. Then ask them what they want to be remembered for.

Tell the Truth

> "Tell truth and shame the devil."
> —*HOTSPUR IN* **HENRY IV** *BY SHAKESPEARE*

Announcer: Welcome, ladies and gentlemen, to "Tell the Truth," the game show where the Spirit of God determines whether the contestants are, indeed, telling the truth. And now our host, Peter!

Peter: Thank you very much. Let's meet today's contestants. We have a husband and wife team, so please join me in welcoming Ananias and Sapphira!

Ananias: Good evening.

Sapphira: Hello.

Peter: OK, now we will take Sapphira offstage and place her in a soundproof box. Ananias, it is time to tell the truth!

Ananias: Uh, OK. So I sold this piece of land, and I would like to give all the proceeds to the church.

Peter: Why did you lie? The Holy Spirit has shown me that you have held some of the money back for yourself. You have not lied to men, but to God!

(Ananias falls down dead and is carried off by some young men.)

Peter: Let's call in Sapphira and hope that she will do better...OK, Sapphira, please tell us: Is this the full amount of money you received for the land?

Sapphira: Yes, it is.

Peter: Why do you test the Spirit of the Lord!? The men who carried out your husband will carry you out as well!

(Sapphira falls down dead and is carried out by some young men.)

Peter: Another tragic story of people who attempted to sneak something past God. If you want to find out all the details about Ananias and Sapphira, you can find them in Acts 5.

Announcer: Thanks, Peter. Once again, friends, we see that a lie is often not just to others, but often to God as well. We are called to be honest and true—and lying always works against that. Strive for honesty, and honor the Spirit of God.

Shall I indicate "lying" as cause of death?

MY THOUGHTS:

> **"The Lord detests lying lips, but he delights in men who are truthful."**
> **—Proverbs 12:22**

MY PRAYERS:

Make a "no lie" pact with your friends. Agree that not only will you be honest with one another, but you will not help your friends lie to anyone else (including parents!).

(Interesting) Ways to Use Your Old Stuff

"The passages in the New Testament...point to God's heaven, God's life, God's dimension... eventually producing new or renewed heavens and new or renewed earth, integrated with each other."
—N. T. Wright

- Arrange old cars in your front yard into a giant modern sculpture.
- Save dryer lint in a plastic bag, and use it to start camp fires.
- Wash out zipper-close plastic bags, and reuse them.
- In the marching band, play an instrument made out of a toilet-paper tube with wax paper rubber-banded to one end.
- Learn to sew and fix your clothes rather than throwing them out.

We hear about the three R's—reduce, reuse, recycle—because they encourage us to care for our planet and be good stewards of our world. You may already participate in local recycling programs or regularly find practical ways to reuse your old stuff. Surprisingly, though, taking care of the earth can be a way for us to remember how God will bring about the "new heavens and new earth" promised in the Scripture.

How? Well, in Romans 8, Paul writes that creation "was subjected to frustration" and "has been groaning as in the pains of childbirth." The renewal of God's creation connects with the renewal of God's covenant with his people. This is explained fully in Romans 5–8 and later reiterated in Revelation 21:1a when John says, "I saw a new heaven and a new earth." In a way, God's redemption of creation is "recycling." He is making everything new! Praise God for his promises and his redemption—both within ourselves and in the future promise of new heavens and earth.

As you recycle or reuse whatever you can, remember God's promises to make *everything* new (and that's a lot of stuff!).

MY THOUGHTS:

"He who was seated on the throne said, 'I am making everything new!' Then he said, 'Write this down, for these words are trustworthy and true.'"
—Revelation 21:5

MY PRAYERS:

What little things can you do to take care of God's creation until God creates a new heaven and earth? Start a new recycling program at your home, school, or church? Fix old things and donate them to thrift stores rather than throwing them out? Make Christmas or birthday gifts?

What's Up With Hell?

"God will never send anybody to hell. If man goes to hell, he goes by his own free choice."
—BILLY GRAHAM

Dear Dr. Doctrine,
Why do non-Christians go to hell? It seems cruel and out of character for a loving God to send people to such a horrible place.
Bewildered

Dear B,

In 1980, a volcano in Washington started rumbling and belching smoke. A report warned that Mount St. Helens was due for a major eruption. Roads were blocked off and people evacuated. Yet few people seemed to grasp the danger. Sightseers streamed to the mountain to gawk and picnic. Loggers kept working so they wouldn't lose money. Planes violated restricted airspace to get a better look, and three hikers climbed the mountain.

After weeks of steam, ash, and earthquakes, almost everyone seemed to be lulled into a false sense of security. Harry Truman, who was 83, was one of the people who refused to leave their homes near the foot of the volcano. "I think the whole thing is over-exaggerated," Truman told reporters. "I've lived here over fifty years. That mountain's part of Harry, and Harry's a part of that mountain."

On May 18, shortly after Mount St. Helens erupted with the force of 500 atomic bombs, Harry Truman and nearly sixty others died because they didn't heed the warnings.

The scientists who warned of the volcano's danger were very concerned for people's safety. They gave ample opportunity for those in danger to avoid disaster. But heeding the warnings was each person's choice.

The reality of hell doesn't mean that God is cruel. Death is the natural consequence of sin. That includes punishment for eternity in hell. But God demonstrates his great love for us in that he warns us and provides a way for us to escape the consequences of our sin. He shouldn't be blamed for being unloving or unfair if we don't take the opportunities he gives us to avoid disaster. People who don't choose to take that way of escape will have to face the natural consequences of their sin. But those who do accept God's great escape plan will enjoy eternal safety and a loving relationship with Jesus!

All the best,
Dr. Doctrine

"How shall we escape if we ignore such a great salvation?"
—Hebrews 2:3

DAILY Challenge™

Think of people you know who have not yet taken God's merciful way of escape from hell through faith in Jesus Christ. Pray for them this week, focusing on one particular person each day. Place one pebble in your pocket for each person, and pray for those people each time you feel the pebbles or become aware of their weight in your pocket. Look for opportunities to tell others about a relationship with Jesus.

The Unknown God

"What is truth?"
—PILATE, DURING JESUS' TRIAL

"For days, this guy, Paul, has been in our city talking about a foreign God. Today, my friends and I decided to ask him about this new teaching. Usually, we spend the whole day talking anyway, so this was exciting because we would have an out-of-towner to share his latest ideas.

"Well, as soon as we asked, he stood up in our meeting place and addressed us all. 'Men of Athens,' he said, 'I've been here a few days, and I have noticed that you're all very religious.' This is true; we're all devoted to many gods. He continued by telling us how he noticed our altar marked 'To an unknown god.' Then he said, 'To you, this god is unknown, but today I'm going to make it known to you!'

"Paul told us that this God is the one who created the whole world and that he cannot be housed in any temple or human-made shrine. Paul said we were God's 'offspring' and that we should repent before the judgment of the world occurs. I guess the strangest thing he talked about was the resurrection of the dead. Our philosophies don't teach that! Every Greek knows the body is what ties us to the horrible material earth! Why would we want a resurrected body? Nevertheless, what he said was so out of the ordinary that some of us told him we'd like to hear more. Others scoffed at what he had to say. Some even decided to believe! I don't know if I'm there yet, but I'm interested in learning more..."

When Paul spoke to the men of Athens, he started with something they were familiar with and understood—the altar to the unknown god. If you read this passage, Acts 17:16-34, you will notice quotations within Paul's sermon. These quotes are from Greek poetry. Paul did not simply stick with the Gospel narrative and stories from the Old Testament; he spoke within the Greek culture.

How can you learn from Paul? How can you find relevance within your culture as you share Jesus?

MY THOUGHTS:

"When they heard about the resurrection of the dead, some of them sneered, but others said, 'We want to hear you again on this subject.' "
—Acts 17:32

MY PRAYERS:

DAILY Challenge™

Look through a magazine, or watch TV for a few minutes. What things do you see that might help you discuss Jesus' story with others? Look for people's needs and references to "higher powers," faith, hope, and love.

Lost Opportunity

My Journal

OCTOBER 20

Hey, God! That youth convention this weekend sparked something in me! I really want to live for you. I want to start loving you by loving others. Show me someone who needs to see your love!

NOVEMBER 21

God, I can't stand this kid. He's just a horrible person. He is so disrespectful and seems to hate everyone. He beat up a kid today for...well, I don't know why. He threatened me today too. Said he'd make it so people don't recognize me. I'm not afraid of him, but it hurts to be hated that much. I'd love to see him pay for the way he treats everyone.

NOVEMBER 22

Oh, yeah...the youth convention last month. But how can you ask us to love people like that, especially when they hate us like this?

DECEMBER 9

I can't do it Lord. He's hopeless—a lost cause. All I did today was say hi to him, and he tripped me with my tray of food in front of the entire cafeteria. That's just about the oldest practical joke in the book. It's dumb. But it was still embarrassing. I give up, God. You're going to have to find someone else to love him. Give me another one.

DECEMBER 17

Christmas break is two days away. I pray, Lord, that he's not in any of my classes next semester. I've tried to talk to him. I know I should try harder. You said it's about you, not about us. But I just can't bring myself to love him for any reason.

JANUARY 8

He didn't come back to school after break. People say he's been missing since Christmas Eve. To be honest, I haven't missed him. I know that's bad, but he's a real loser. I'm sorry, God. I really tried. You saw that, right?

FEBRUARY 27

His body was found in the woods behind school. He had a gun in his hand. Suicide, they say. I can't believe the pain he must have been suffering. Through that hard shell of a person, a hurting soul needed someone to care, someone who would just listen to him. Maybe if I had spent a few minutes paying closer attention to him instead of trying to avoid him, this wouldn't have happened. Maybe he would have had a chance to see you. You were right, Lord. I needed to love him for you. Everyone is so numb. Even though he's been missing for a couple months, it carves a new hole. Not only is a person missing, a life was lost. Lord, help me love others the way you do.

"In spite of everything I still believe that people are really good at heart."
—ANNE FRANK

Write down the name of someone who needs to feel God's love through you. Put that name somewhere so you will be reminded to pray for that person and develop a relationship with him or her.

MY THOUGHTS:

"For we do not preach ourselves, but Jesus Christ as Lord, and ourselves as your servants for Jesus' sake."
—2 Corinthians 4:5

MY PRAYERS:

Is That You?

God has done some great things through me. I'm sure you have heard of some of them. People may say that I, Elijah, did them. It was really God. But something went wrong. God just seemed to leave me. People were not listening to me. In fact, they were trying to kill me. I was working so hard for the Lord, and it seemed as if he left me. I was tired of struggling and came to this desolate place to get away.

Then, today, God told me to stand on this mountain and wait for him. So I waited for him to show up, and some amazing things happened!

First, there was a huge windstorm. The wind was so strong that it split rocks. I was sure it was God. It seems like a God thing, doesn't it? But it wasn't him. Next, there was a tremendous earthquake. God is certainly capable of shaking the earth. But it wasn't him. Finally, there was a raging fire. Huge flames and smoke billowed high in the sky. "There you are," I thought. But it wasn't him. I was confused. These were the ways God had showed himself before.

Just as I was about to leave, I heard this gentle voice speaking to me. The voice wanted to know why I was in the wilderness. I told the voice everything I've told you. The sound of my words seemed empty. But this gentle voice resonated in my ears and my heart. The voice gave me peace. I remembered many times when God's gentle presence had given me hope.

I finally understood. God had not left me; I just wasn't listening. He is the ever-present and gentle voice that speaks to my heart and gives me peace and strength.

I have to go now, but thanks for listening. I will keep up the work because I know he is always with me. (You can find this story in 1 Kings 19:1-18.)

"He works on us in all sorts of ways: not only through what we think our 'religious life.'"
—C.S. LEWIS

Day & Night

I'M WITH YOU Always

MY THOUGHTS:

"And surely I am with you always, to the very end of the age."
—Matthew 28:20

MY PRAYERS:

DAILY Challenge™

Listen to the sounds around you, and answer these questions.
- What is the gentlest sound?
- What noises can you filter out to hear the gentle sound better?
- What life-noises can you filter out so you can hear God's voice better?

"**prej·u·dice 1a.** An adverse judgment or opinion formed beforehand or without knowledge or examination of the facts. **b.** A preconceived preference or idea. **2.** The act or state of holding unreasonable preconceived judgments or convictions. **3.** Irrational suspicion or hatred of a particular group, race, or religion. **4.** Detriment or injury caused to a person by the preconceived, unfavorable conviction of another or others."
–*American Heritage Dictionary of the English Language: Fourth Edition*

Prejudice Is a Drag

Have you ever been treated differently because of how you look, where you're from, or what you can or can't do? It's so hard to deal with people who judge you or don't take the time to get to know you and see your great worth.

Prejudice isn't a new thing. We see examples of it even in biblical times. For instance, in Exodus 1, Pharaoh gave an order to have all baby boys killed and let all baby girls live. In John 1:46, Nathanael learned that Jesus was from Nazareth. Nathanael said, "Nazareth! Can anything good come from there?" And Genesis 43:32 explains that Egyptians and Hebrews didn't eat together because Egyptians considered it "detestable" to eat with Hebrews.

The Bible also gives advice about dealing with prejudice. It's not always easy to rise above the hurt it causes. But here are some passages that might help you better understand what God wants our response to be.

• "You have heard that it was said, 'Love your neighbor and hate your enemy.' But I tell you: Love your enemies and pray for those who persecute you, that you may be sons of your Father in heaven" (Matthew 5:43-45).

• "Do not repay anyone evil for evil. Be careful to do what is right in the eyes of everybody. If it is possible, as far as it depends on you, live at peace with everyone. Do not take revenge, my friends, but leave room for God's wrath, for it is written: 'It is mine to avenge; I will repay,' says the Lord...Do not be overcome by evil, but overcome evil with good" (Romans 12:17-19, 21).

God wants our response to be Christlike in every situation: when we're treated unfairly, discriminated against, and persecuted. It's hard to do, but it's important to love people the way Jesus loved us. He loved us even though we were sinners, and it changed our lives forever. To carry that message to others through our love could change their lives too.

MY THOUGHTS:

"Righteousness and justice are the foundation of your throne; love and faithfulness go before you."
–Psalm 89:14

MY PRAYERS:

Create a brief "mission statement" that addresses your feelings about prejudice and how you can counteract it with your life. Tape it on your mirror so you'll always be reminded to be a positive influence against prejudice of any kind.

The Price of Freedom

Ever heard of San Francisco? Ever seen a little statue in your neighbor's garden of a monk feeding the birds? Why do you keep answering strange questions? Both the city and the statue are based on St. Francis, a monk in the Middle Ages who began to change the world when he was young.

The story goes that Francis came back from the military but didn't want to be a soldier. His father was a rich tailor, but he didn't want to be a merchant. Instead, he heard God call him to rebuild a monastery that was in ruins. Apparently, Francis took off his clothes in the middle of a public square and handed them to his father, telling him that he was returning his possessions. Francis then went to live a life of poverty and service, rebuilding the monastery. Soon, other men joined him, and the movement spread. In 1209, the pope declared the Franciscans to be a new monastic order, and Franciscan monasteries spread throughout Europe.

Francis emphasized that we must abandon worldly wealth to serve God, as Jesus taught. No one was allowed to join Francis until he or she had sold all personal possessions and given the money to the poor. Throughout his life, Francis owned nothing more than a simple cloak to wear. He gave all his money to helping the poor.

Ironically, Francis gained everything he wanted (and what most of us want!) by giving everything away. Francis received the gift of eternal life through a relationship with Jesus and went on to change the entire world. Hundreds of people were directly affected by his life, and millions more have read his story and simplified their lives as a result. By giving up the world, Francis was used by God to bless the world. Even today, his story has the power to change the life of someone who simply reads a devotional about him.

"Lord, make me an instrument of Your peace! Where there is hatred let me sow love...Where there is darkness, light; Where there is sadness, joy."
—ST. FRANCIS OF ASSISI

MY THOUGHTS:

"Do not love the world or anything in the world. If anyone loves the world, the love of the Father is not in him."
—1 John 2:15

MY PRAYERS:

Take a dollar bill to the highest or windiest place you can find. Let it go. Think about what it means to let go of material things in this world. Pray that God would give you real freedom.

"If there are some ambiguities for us as to how *all the details are to work out, there is no ambiguity as to the certainty that God* will *work it all out–in his time and in his way."*
–GORDON D. FEE

Can't Wait!

It was the last day of school, and Tara hardly had the patience to clean out her locker and return her books. As she ran outside, backpack unzipped, all she could think about was *the lake.* Every summer for fifteen years, Tara had flown to Minnesota, where she spent two glorious months with her dad and grandparents at the lake home. Tara loved to canoe in the morning, and, in the afternoon, her dad would drive the ski boat while she flew behind it. But this year, Dad had told her that he would teach her how to drive the boat. Tara couldn't wait! She couldn't wait to leave Arizona, see her grandparents and Dad, and hurtle off the dock into the bright blue water.

Charlie sat on the couch, watching the second hand on the grandfather clock in the parlor. "Forty-seven minutes before this seventy-two-hour grounding is over," he thought. He brushed the fibers of the sofa upholstery so that they stood up, and then he smoothed them back down. He looked at the clock–forty-six minutes. He sighed.

Krista raised her arms. "OK, everyone, be quiet! Michael said he'd try to have Jill here by 6:30, and it's 6:27. Find a place to hide, and then right after she comes into the door, shout 'Surprise!' " Krista double-checked the cake, snacks, and candles and then ducked into the broom closet.

What do Tara, Charlie, and Krista have in common? They're all waiting for something–something good. Tara has to wait ten months every year to go to the lake, Charlie has to wait seventy-two hours for his punishment to be over, and Krista has to wait three minutes to spring a birthday surprise on a friend.

For two thousand years, the church has been waiting for Christ's promised return. Though there is a multitude of ways to explain what will happen, Christians all agree on one thing: One day, Christ will return. We may respond differently–apprehension, excitement, daydreams–but we do (and should) look forward to the great finale of God's story. How are you spending your time waiting for Jesus to return?

MY THOUGHTS:

"He who testifies to these things says, 'Yes, I am coming soon.' "
–Revelation 22:20

MY PRAYERS:

DAILY Challenge™

What sorts of things in your life discourage you? How can hope in the return of Christ help encourage your walk with God? Jot down things that encourage you and remind you to be excited for Christ's return.